THE GREATNESS GUIDE

ALSO BY ROBIN SHARMA

MegaLiving

The Monk Who Sold His Ferrari

Leadership Wisdom from the Monk Who Sold His Ferrari

Who Will Cry When You Die?

Family Wisdom from the Monk Who Sold His Ferrari

The Saint, the Surfer and the CEO

Discover Your Destiny with the Monk Who Sold His Ferrari

ROBIN SHARMA
THE GREATNESS GUIDE

ONE OF THE WORLD'S TOP SUCCESS COACHES
SHARES HIS SECRETS FOR PERSONAL
AND BUSINESS MASTERY

HarperCollins*Publishers*Ltd

The Greatness Guide
© 2006 by Robin S. Sharma.
All rights reserved.

Published by HarperCollins*PublishersLtd.*

First edition

HarperCollins books may be purchased for
educational, business, or sales promotional
use through our Special Markets Department.

HarperCollins*PublishersLtd.*
2 Bloor Street East, 20th Floor
Toronto, Ontario, Canada
M4W 1A8

www.harpercollins.ca

Library and Archives Canada Cataloguing in
Publication

Sharma, Robin S. (Robin Shilp), 1964–
The greatness guide : the 10 best lessons life
has taught me / Robin Sharma.

ISBN-13: 978-0-00-200730-6
ISBN-10: 0-00-200730-4

1. Success. 2. Self-actualization (Psychology).
3. Sharma, Robin S.

(Robin Shilp), 1964-. I. Title.

BF637.S4S47 2006   158.1
C2005-905593-6

h c 9 8 7

Printed and bound in the United States
Set in ITC New Baskerville

I dedicate this book, with deep respect and great love, to my parents. You not only gave me the gift of life but an unrelenting passion to live it fully. For that I am so very grateful.

Contents

*"Life is pure adventure and the sooner we realize that,
the quicker we will be able to treat life as art."*

Maya Angelou

*"I used to think that one day I'd be able to resolve the different
drives I have in different directions, the tensions between the
different people I am. Now I realize that is who I am. I do feel I'm
getting closer to the song in my head. I wasn't looking for grace.
But luckily grace was looking for me."*

Bono, lead singer of U2, as quoted in *Rolling Stone*

1

I'm No Guru

The media sometimes calls me a leadership (or self-help) "guru." I'm not. I'm just an ordinary guy who happens to have learned ideas and tools that have helped many human beings reach their best lives and many organizations get to world class.

But I must be really clear: I'm no different from you. I have my struggles, my frustrations and my own fears—along with my hopes, goals and dreams. I've had good seasons and some deeply painful ones. I've made some spectacularly good choices and some outrageously bad mistakes. I'm very human—a work in progress. If I have ideas that you find insightful, please know it's simply because I spend my days focused on the knowledge you are about to experience. Thinking about practical ways to help you play your biggest game as a human being and reach greatness. Dwelling on how I can help companies get to the extraordinary. Do anything long enough and you'll get some depth of insight and understanding about it. Then they'll call you a guru.

A man at a signing I did at a bookstore in Bangalore, India, heard me say, "I'm no guru." He came up to me and said: "Why are you so uncomfortable being called a guru? 'Gu' simply means 'darkness' in Sanskrit and 'ru' simple means 'dispel.' So the word 'guru' simply speaks of one who dispels the darkness and brings more understanding and light." Nice point. Made me think.

I've had good seasons and some deeply painful ones. I've made some **spectacularly** good choices and some outrageously bad mistakes. I'm **very** human—a work in progress.

I guess my discomfort stems from the fact that if you think I'm different from you, then you might say, "Well, I can't do the kinds of things Robin talks about because he has talents and abilities I don't have. All the stuff he talks about is easy for him to do. He's this guru." Nope. Sorry to disappoint you. I'm just a guy working hard to make the best of his days, trying to be a great single dad to my two wonderful children and hoping he's—in some way—making a difference in peoples' lives. No guru here. But I do like the "dispelling the darkness" point. Need to learn more about that one. Maybe some guru can help me.

2

Harvey Keitel and Windows of Opportunity

I don't always get it right (I told you I'm no guru). But please know that I try so hard to walk my talk and to ensure my video is in alignment with my audio. Still, I am a human being, and that means sometimes I slip (I've yet to meet a perfect one). Here's what I mean.

I spend a lot of time encouraging the readers of my books and the participants at my workshops on personal and organizational leadership to "run toward your fears" and to seize those "cubic centimeters of chance" (opportunities) when they present themselves. I challenge my clients to dream, to shine and to dare, because to me a life well lived is all about reaching for your highest and your best. And, in my mind, the person who experiences the most wins. Most of the time, I am a poster boy for visiting the places that scare me and doing the things that make me feel uncomfortable. But recently, I didn't. Sorry.

I was downtown at the Four Seasons in Toronto, in the lobby getting ready for a speech I was about to give to a company called Advanced Medical Optics, which is a long-standing

leadership coaching client of ours and an impressive organization. I look up and guess who I see? Harvey Keitel. Yes, the
Harvey "*Reservoir Dogs* Big Movie Star" Keitel. And what does
the man who wrote *The Monk Who Sold His Ferrari* do? I shrink
from greatness.

Each day, life will send you little windows of opportunity. Your **destiny** will ultimately be defined by how you **respond** to these windows of opportunity.

I don't know why I didn't stand up and walk over and
make a new friend. I've done it with baseball legend Pete Rose
at the Chicago airport (we ended up sitting next to each other
all the way to Phoenix). I did it last summer with Henry Kravis,
one of the planet's top financiers in the lobby of a hotel in Rome
(I was with my kids, and Colby, my 11-year-old son, thought he
was pretty cool). I did it with Senator Edward Kennedy when I
saw him in Boston. I even did it with guitar virtuoso Eddie Van
Halen when I was a kid growing up in Halifax, Nova Scotia. But
I missed the chance to connect with Harvey Keitel.

Each day, life will send you little windows of opportunity.
Your destiny will ultimately be defined by how you respond to
these windows of opportunity. Shrink from them and your life
will be small. Feel the fear and run to them anyway, and your life
will be big. Life's just too short to play little. Even with your kids,
you only have a tiny window to develop them and champion

their highest potential. And to show them what unconditional love looks like. When that window closes, it's hard to reopen it.

If I see Harvey Keitel again, I promise you that I'll sprint toward him. He may think I'm a celebrity stalker until we start to chat. And then he'll discover the truth: I'm simply a man who seizes the gifts that life presents to him.

3

Nothing Fails like Success

Richard Carrion, the CEO of Puerto Rico's top bank, once shared a line with me that I'll never forget: "Robin, nothing fails like success." Powerful thought. You, as well as your organization, are most vulnerable when you are most successful. Success actually breeds complacency, inefficiency and—worst of all—arrogance. When people and businesses get really successful, they often fall in love with themselves. They stop innovating, working hard, taking risks and begin to rest on their laurels. They go on the defensive, spending their energy protecting their success rather than staying true to the very things that got them to the top. Whenever I share this point with a roomful of CEOs, every single one of them nods in agreement. Please let me give you a real-world example from my own life.

This past weekend, I took my kids to our favorite Italian restaurant. The food is incredible there. The best bresaola outside of Italy. Heavenly pasta. Super foamy lattes that make me want to give up my job and become a barista. But the service at this place is bad. Bad, bad, bad (like it is at most places). Why? Because the place is always full. And because they are doing so well, they've taken the lines out front for granted. And guess what? It's the beginning of their end.

I love taking pictures. My dad taught me to record the journey of my life with photos. So I generally carry a little camera around with me. I asked our server if she would snap a picture of my children and me as we dug into our spaghetti. "I don't have time" was the curt reply. Unbelievable. Too busy to take five seconds to keep a customer happy. Too busy to help out a little. Too busy to show some humanity.

The more successful you and your organization become, the more humble and devoted to your customers you need to be.

"Nothing fails like success." Richard Carrion gets it. So does David Neeleman, the CEO of JetBlue, who observed: "When you're making money and good margins, you tend to get sloppy." Many CEOs don't. The more successful you and your organization become, the more humble and devoted to your customers you need to be. The more committed to efficiency and relentless improvement you need to be. The faster you need to play. The more value you need to add. Because the moment you stop doing the very things that got you to the top of the mountain is the very moment you begin the slide down to the valley.

4

Be a Rock Star at Work

Just finished reading an article in *Fortune* on the Google guys and all their economic success. It inspired a torrent of ideas (reading's like that, isn't it?). It got me thinking about the importance of showing up fully at work—giving the fullness of your brilliance and playing full out. Being wildly passionate about your To Do's. Being breathtakingly committed to your big projects and best opportunities. Being a rock star in whatever you do each day to put bread on your table.

Work gives meaning to our lives. It influences our self-worth and the way we perceive our place under the sun. Being great at what you do isn't just something you do for the organization you work for—it's a gift you give yourself. Being spectacularly great at your work promotes personal respect, excitement and just makes your life a lot more interesting. Good things happen to people who do good things. And when you bring your highest talents and deepest devotion to the work you do, what you are really doing is setting yourself up for a richer, happier and more fulfilling experience of living.

How do you feel after an ultra-productive day? How do you feel when you've given your best, had fun with your teammates and gone the extra mile for customers? How do you feel when you've brought more heart to what you do for a living? How do you feel when you reached for your greatest goals and grabbed them? It feels pretty good, doesn't it? And you don't need to have the biggest title to do the best job. This point makes me think of the words of Dr. Martin Luther King Jr.—one of my heroes—who once observed: "If a man is called to be a street sweeper, he should sweep streets even as Michelangelo painted, or as Beethoven composed music or Shakespeare wrote poetry. He should sweep streets so well that all the hosts of heaven and earth will pause to say, 'here lived a great street sweeper who did his job well.'"

And you don't need to have the biggest title to do the best job.

So be a rock star at work today. Walk onto the stage of this day and play your heart out. Give the performance of your life. Wow your audience and get them cheering for you. Be the Bono of selling staplers. Be the Keith Richards of accounting. Be the Jimi Hendrix of human resources. And when you get famous and people from all over ask you for your autograph, make sure you drop me a line. I'd love to hear from you.

$$\boxed{5}$$

Your Days Define Your Life

Big idea: Your days are your life in miniature. As you live your hours, so you create your years. As you live your days, so you craft your life. What you do today is actually creating your future. The words you speak, the thoughts you think, the food you eat and the actions you take are defining your destiny—shaping who you are becoming and what your life will stand for. Small choices lead to giant consequences—over time. There's no such thing as an unimportant day.

As you live your days, so you craft your life.

Each one of us is called to greatness. Each one of us has an exquisite power within us. Each one of us can have a significant impact on the world around us—if we so choose. But for this power that resides internally to grow, we need to use it. And the more you exercise it, the stronger it gets. The more this power gets tapped, the more confident you become. Henry David Thoreau related to this point well when he wrote: "I know of no more encouraging fact than the unquestionable ability of a human being to elevate their life by conscious endeavor." And advertising guru Donny Deutsch added a more current spin on the idea when he wrote in his book *Often Wrong, Never in Doubt*: "For every person with the stuff, the one out of a hundred who goes to a rarefied place is the one who says, 'why not me?' and goes for it."

The best among us are not more gifted than the rest. They just take little steps each day as they march toward their biggest life. And the days slip into weeks, the weeks into months and before they know it, they arrive at a place called Extraordinary.

6

Drink Coffee with Gandhi

Reading is one of the best disciplines I know of to stay "on your game" and at your highest. Reading from a great book is really all about having a conversation with the author. And we become our conversations. Just think, tonight—by reading Mahatma Gandhi's autobiography, *My Experiments with Truth*, over a cup of coffee—you can get behind this great man's eyeballs and learn what made him tick. Want to hang out with Madonna tomorrow? Grab her book. Same for Jack Welch, Mother Teresa, Bill Gates, Salvador Dali or the Dalai Lama. And reading a book by someone you respect allows some of their brilliance to rub off on you. The hand that puts down a great book will never be the same. As Oliver Wendell Holmes observed: "A mind once stretched by a new idea can never return to its original dimensions."

When I was growing up my father once told me: "Cut back on your rent or cut back on what you spend on food but never worry about investing money in a good book." That powerful thought has accompanied me through life. His philosophy was that all it takes is one idea discovered in a single book to lift you to a whole new level and revolutionize the way you see the world. And so our home was filled with books. And now I try to devote at least an hour a day to reading. That habit alone has transformed me. Thank you, Dad.

Perhaps my greatest gift to my children when I die will be my library. I have books on leadership, relationships, business, philosophy, wellness, spirituality, great lives and many of my other favored topics in it. Many of these I've picked up in bookshops from across the planet when I travel on business. These books have shaped my thinking. They have formed my personal philosophy. They have made me the man I am. To me, my books are priceless.

Reading a book by someone you respect allows some of their brilliance to rub off on you.

The old expression is true: "Knowing how to read and not reading is almost the same as not knowing how to read." Make the time to read something good each day. Fill your mind with big ideas and dazzling thoughts. Use books to flood your soul with hope and inspiration. And remember, if you want to lead, you really need to read. Oh, and if you—like me—have the habit of buying more books than you can ever possibly read, don't feel guilty—you're building your library. And that's a beautiful thing.

7

Get Some Skin in the Game

I fail more than most people. I fail all the time. I've had failures in business. I've had failures in relationships. I've had failures in life. I used to wonder why this happened. I used to play Poor Me and suffer from the dreaded disease of victimitis infinitus. But now I get it. I've been stumbling toward my best life. Failure is the price of greatness. Failure is an essential ingredient for a high achievement. As innovation guru David Kelley wrote: "Fail faster. Succeed sooner." You can't win without leaving your safety zone and taking some calculated risks. No risk, no reward. And the more risks you take in the pursuit of your dreams, the more you are going to fail.

Too many among us live in what I call the safe harbor of the known. Same breakfast for 20 years. Same drive to work for 20 years. Same conversations for 20 years. Same thinking for 20 years. I have no judgment on that kind of a life. If it makes you happy, well, that's great. But I don't know of anyone who is happy living like that. If you keep doing what you've been doing, you'll keep getting what you've been getting. Einstein defined insanity as doing the same things but expecting different results. Yet most people rule their lives that way. True joy comes when you put some skin in the game and take some chances. Yes, you will start to experience more failure. But guess what? Success also starts to pay more visits.

Failure is just part of the process of getting to world class. "Screw-ups are the mark of excellence," said management consultant Tom Peters. The best companies on the planet have failed more than the average ones. The most successful people on the planet have failed more than ordinary ones. To me, the only failure is the failure to try and dream and dare. The real risk lies in riskless living. Mark Twain made the point perfectly when he observed: "Twenty years from now you will be more disappointed by the things you didn't do than by the ones you did."

The real risk lies in riskless living.

So go ahead, stretch today. Ask for the best table in your favorite restaurant. Ask for an upgrade to first class on your next flight (good luck). Ask your teammate at work for more understanding. Ask your sweetheart at home for more love. Do it. I dare you. And remember, you can't win a game that you don't even play.

8

Be into Breezes

I was at my tennis club a while ago with my kids, who are great players. I'm a great ball boy at best. A man who I guess would be in his early seventies comes up to me and starts a conversation. Interesting person. Lived a rich life so far. After a few moments, he closes his eyes and smiles. I ask: "What's going on?" His reply was unforgettable: "Oh, nothing much. It's just that I'm really into breezes." Perfect.

Some of life's best pleasures are its simplest ones. Enrich your life with more of them and your heart will be happy.

In this age of wanting more, needing more and having more, it was so refreshing to hear someone speak of the simple pleasures of life. I need to be clear: I have nothing against material things. Contrary to popular belief, *The Monk Who Sold His Ferrari* isn't a manifesto against making money and enjoying the good life. My main message there was simply "remember what's

most important to leading a great life." Drive a BMW, wear
Prada, stay at the Four Seasons and earn a ton of money if these
are things that make you happy. Life is certainly full of material
pleasures that really do make the journey more delightful. No
need to feel guilty about enjoying them. But please don't forget
about those basic but beautiful treasures to be loved along the
way. Like deep human connections, realizing your best through
fulfilling work, exploring the world and experiencing the glory
of nature—like a sensational sunset that fills your soul or a full
moon set against a star-filled sky.

Some of life's best pleasures are its simplest ones. Enrich
your life with more of them and your heart will be happy. And
you can start with sweet breezes.

9

Make Time to Think

I am blessed to be able to meet interesting people from all walks of life regularly because of the work I do. I meet film-makers, poets, brilliant college students, wise teachers and visionary entrepreneurs. Each one of these encounters has taught me something and shaped my perspective. I had dinner recently with one of Asia's top CEOs. Asked him the secret of his outrageous success. He smiled: "I make the time to think." Every morning, he spends at least 45 minutes with his eyes closed, deep in reflection. He's not meditating. He's not pray-ing. He's thinking.

Sometimes he's analyzing business challenges. Other times he's thinking about new markets. Still other times he's being introspective on the meaning of his life and what he wants it to stand for. Often, he's simply dreaming up new ways to grow per-sonally and professionally. Every once in a while, he'll spend between six and eight hours doing this. Sitting silently. Still. With his eyes closed. Thinking.

Making the time to think is a superb strategy for success at leadership and in life. Too many people spend the best hours of their days solely engaged in doing, on the execution aspect of things. Recently a client said to me: "Robin, sometimes I get so busy that I don't even know what I'm so busy doing." But what if he's busy with the wrong things? Few things are as disappointing as investing all your time, energy and potential climbing a mountain only to find—once at the top—that you climbed the wrong one. Thinking and reflection ensures that you're on the right mountain. Peter Drucker, the management expert, said it so well: "There is nothing so useless as doing efficiently that which should not be done at all."

Peter Drucker, the management expert, said it so well: "There is nothing so useless as doing efficiently that which should not be done at all."

Being thoughtful and strategic is step number one as you walk to greatness. Clarity precedes success. By thinking more, you will have a better sense of your priorities and what you need to focus on. Your actions will be more crisp and deliberate and intentional. You will make better decisions and wiser choices. More time thinking will make you less reactive. You'll become clearer on the best uses of your time (which will, in turn, save you time). And your "think time" will provoke some amazing ideas and inspire some big dreams. Lewis Carroll addressed this point beautifully in *Alice in Wonderland* when he wrote:

"'There's no use in trying,' said Alice. 'One can't believe impossible things.' 'I daresay you haven't had much practice,' said the Queen. 'When I was your age, I always did it for half an hour a day. Why sometimes I've believed as many as six impossible things before breakfast.'"

10

Leadership Begins on the Extra Mile

I had just dropped off Colby and Bianca at school and was driving to the office when I got an insight that made me pull over. So here I sit, off to the side of the road with my hazard blinkers on, hammering this out on my BlackBerry because I wanted to share it with you. The big idea: Leadership—and success—*begins* on the extra mile.

Ordinary people don't spend much time on the extra mile. But who ever said you were ordinary?

Leadership is shown when a salesperson makes extra calls at the end of an exhausting day—not because it's the easy thing to do but because it's the right thing to do. Leadership is shown by the manager who finishes a report that has taken the very best from him, then goes back to it a little later to polish and improve it even more. Leadership is shown by a team that delivers on their value promise to a customer and then digs even deeper to wow them. And leadership is shown by the human being who fights the urge to stay under the covers on a cold day and throws on her running shoes to pound the pavement. Not because running miles on a frosty morning is fun. But because it's wise.

Please think about this idea. I think it's a deeply important one. Those among us who craft extraordinary careers and spectacular lives are those who spend most of their time giving their best out on the extra mile. Yes, ordinary people don't spend much time on the extra mile. But who ever said you were ordinary?

11

Mick Jagger
and Reference Points

Last Monday night I watched a 62-year-old man rock the house for more than two hours in front of 30,000 adoring fans. Yup, Mick is 62 and the once young Stones frontman is aging. But he still has that charisma. Still has the moves. Still has the youth.

As I watched him, I thought of a term I've been sharing at my seminars these days: "reference points." I heard someone say last week: "I'm in my sixties—getting near the end of my life." Not if Mick is your reference point.

Positive reference points will pull you into a new way of seeing things and introduce you to a new set of possibilities. Doors you never even knew existed will begin to open. Lance Armstrong is a great reference point on persistence. My father is a great reference point on integrity. My mother is an excellent reference point on kindness. My children are superb reference points on what unconditional love and boundless curiosity look like. Richard Branson is a spectacular reference point on living a full-out life. Madonna is a great reference point on reinvention.

Peter Drucker was a wonderful reference point on the importance of lifelong learning. Nelson Mandela is a brilliant reference point on courage and humanitarianism.

Often, we have weak reference points so we see the limitations of a scenario rather than the opportunities. With world-
class reference points, you will realize far more of your potential
and life will have more wonder. You will play a bigger game as a
human being if you pick the right people to model. We are all
cut from the same cloth. We are all flesh and bones. If they can
get to greatness—so can you. You just need to do the same kinds
of things your reference points did to reach their excellence.

Positive reference points will pull you into a new way of seeing things and introduce you to a new set of possibilities. Doors you never even knew existed will begin to open.

And I'll tell you one thing: When I'm 62, I want to be like
Mick. Because he's just getting started.

12

Business Is Relationships

I'm sitting on a plane in Frankfurt as I write this chapter. I spent yesterday meeting with publishers who have distributed *The Monk Who Sold His Ferrari* series around the world. Each autumn, Frankfurt comes alive as 250,000 publishing people descend on the city for the world's largest book fair. For me, today marks the last day of a 20-day speaking and book tour that took me throughout India (one of my favorite countries to visit) to Istanbul (a fantastic place) and finally to this small German city. Learned so much these past three weeks. Met so many amazing human beings who blessed me with their kindness. Been moved by the sea change of people who are reaching for their greatest lives and leading by example. Perhaps most of all, I've been reminded that few things are more important than building relationships.

How easy it is to forget that, ultimately, business and life is all about forging human bonds. Being out on this tour, I laughed with my readers at book signings. I broke bread with the clients we do leadership development work for. I drank coffee with my publishers. I got to know the people in this community that has grown around my message. And they got to know me.

Big idea: People want to know that you are real. That you

are decent, kind and trustworthy. They want to feel you and sense you and look into your eyes to see what you are made of. They want to know your passion for whatever it is you stand for. And when they sense that you are the real deal, they will open up to you. When they see that you have their best interests in mind, they will trust you—and keep your best interests in mind. Once they get that you are good, they'll be good to you. And your career (along with your life) will get to a place called world class based on those trust connections. It's easy to forget that people do business with people they like—and who make them feel good. Simple stuff—I know. Yet most of us just don't get around to becoming masterful at the basics. Success is all about consistency around the fundamentals. The only thing that's rocket science is rocket science.

It's easy to forget that people do business with people they like.

So I invite you to get out of your office and go circulate. Being out there makes good things happen. Nothing really happens until you move. Shake hands. Do lunches. Show genuine interest. Spread your goodwill. Evangelize your message. Remember that before someone will lend you a hand, you need to touch their heart. And that business is all about relationships.

13

Life Lessons from SpongeBob SquarePants

SpongeBob SquarePants is my hero. The kids and I were having breakfast this morning when Bianca, my nine-year-old daughter, brought up the subject of this crazy little cartoon character. "Daddy, is SpongeBob a real person?" Made me laugh. Then it made me think. If SpongeBob were a human being, this world would be a better place. Seriously. Here are four lessons SpongeBob can teach us to get more joy from life:

BE THE ETERNAL OPTIMIST. *The guy (or sponge, I should say) always sees the best in any situation. Your thinking really does shape your reality. And because SpongeBob looks for the best, he finds it.*

VALUE PEOPLE. *SpongeBob knows what friendship means. He loves his pals in Bikini Bottom, even Squidword "who is always cranky," to borrow my son's words. SpongeBob knows that respect and putting people first are two of the most important elements for strong relationships.*

BE AN ORIGINAL. *SpongeBob is one of a kind. Too many among us are afraid to be ourselves. So we give up our dreams to follow the crowd. Tragic. "To thine own self be true," wrote Shakespeare. Have the courage to be your true—and greatest—you. (Warren Buffett, chairman of Berkshire Hathaway, once said, "There can't be two yous.")*

Too many among us are afraid to be ourselves. So we give up our dreams to follow the crowd.

LAUGH AND HAVE FUN. *There's no point in being successful but sad. Makes no sense. Yes, reach for the mountaintop. But enjoy the climb as well. Life wasn't meant to be an ordeal. It was meant to be a celebration. So have big-time fun as you chase—and catch—your most cherished dreams.*

14

How to Be a Happier Human

Here's a simple idea that has worked brilliantly for the executives and entrepreneurs who I coach: If you want to be happier, do more of the things that make you happy. I know that seems like an obvious point—but it's not. As we leave the wonder years of childhood, most of us stop doing the things that make our hearts sing. One CEO client told me recently that when he was young, he used to love to take long solo rides on his bicycle. "I stopped doing that when we had kids and work demands took over. Life just got busier. But those moments out on that bike came from some of the best days of my life." Another client, a phenomenally successful entrepreneur, shared that his passion used to be playing his drums in a rock band. "Those were incredible times. Then I started my business and it began to consume me. I miss playing music. I'd lose myself in it."

Here's your To Do: Make a list of your 10 Greatest Passions, 10 activities that fill your heart with joy and remind you of how good life can be. And then, over the coming 10 weeks, inject one of those pursuits into your weekly schedule. Powerful thought: The things that get scheduled are the things that get done. Until you schedule something, it's only a concept—and extraordinary people don't build remarkable lives on concepts.

They build their greatness on action and near-flawless execution around their deliverables. They get things done.

This 10-week program works. When you get back to doing those things that lifted your spirit and sent you soaring, you reconnect with that state of happiness that you may have lost. And part of the purpose of life is to be happy. Really happy.

When you get back to doing those things that lifted your spirit and sent you soaring, you reconnect with that state of happiness that you may have lost.

15

Work Hard, Get Lucky

That old line remains so true: "The harder I work, the luckier I get." Life helps those who help themselves. Learned that one from personal experience. I'm not one of those New Age types that believes "it's all meant to be" and that our lives have been scripted by an invisible set of hands. That kind of talk smacks of "victimspeak" and fear. Fear of failure. Fear of rejection. Fear of not being good enough. Fear of success. That kind of language also lacks any sense of personal responsibility and usually comes from people too afraid to get into the game. Sure I believe that there's a force of nature that comes into play when we least expect it (and most need it). And yes, I believe there is a coherence to the way our lives unfold that is highly intelligent. But I also believe—deeply—that we were given free will and the power to make choices for a single reason: to exercise them. I believe that we generally get from life what we give to life. I believe that good things happen to those willing to put in the effort, exercise discipline and make the sacrifices that personal and professional greatness requires—no, demands. I've also found that actions have consequences and the more good things I do—through good old hard work—the more success I see. Life favors the devoted.

Not one of the über-successful people I've worked with as a leadership coach got there without outworking everyone around them. While others were home watching TV or sleeping, these great ones—who have made their mark on the world and have added tremendous value to it—were up early, putting in the hours, showing life that they were dedicated to their dream. I'm not—for even a moment—denying the importance of work-life balance and spending time with loved ones or caring for your inner life. I'll be the first to stand for those values. All I'm saying is that behind extraordinary achievement you will always discover extraordinary effort. Just a law of nature. Hasn't changed for a thousand years.

Not one of the über-successful people I've worked with as a leadership coach got there without outworking everyone around them.

Ivan Seidenberg, the chairman and CEO of Verizon, tells the following story: "My first boss—he was the building superintendent and I was a janitor—watched me sweep floors and wash walls for almost a year before he mentioned I could get tuition for college if I got a job with the phone company. When I asked him why he waited so long, he said: 'I wanted to see if you were worth it.'"

And Time Warner CEO Dick Parsons once observed that the best advice he ever got was from his grandmother. She told him: "Whatever a man soweth, that shall he also reap." So plant your seeds. Be spectacularly great at what you do. Wear your passion on your sleeve and hold your heart in the palm of your hand. And work hard. Really hard. Hard work opens doors and shows the world that you are serious about being one of those rare—and special—human beings that uses the fullness of their talents for the highest and the very best.

16

Know Your Genius

Genius is not the sole domain of a rare breed of person. Both you and I are entitled to that label and to play in that space—if we so choose. Here's the big idea: Focus on any area or skill with a relentless devotion to daily improvement and a passion for excellence and within three to five years, you will be operating at a level of competence (and insight) such that people call you a genius. Focus plus daily improvement plus time equals genius. Understand that formula deeply and your life will never be the same.

Michael Jordan was a basketball genius. Was his spectacular success on the court purely the result of natural gifts? Absolutely not. He took what nature gave him and ran the formula: Focus plus daily improvement plus time equals genius. He didn't try to be good at five different sports. He didn't scatter his focus. He just got devoted to being brilliant at basketball. And he was.

Thomas Edison registered a stunning 1093 patents over his lifetime and invented the light bulb as well as the phonograph. (A schoolteacher labelled him a slow learner when he was a kid; he didn't listen. Kudos.) He didn't try to be a great merchant and a great poet and a great musician. He focused on his inventions. He improved daily. And he let time work its magic. Genius came knocking.

Makes me think of a story about Pablo Picasso. One day a woman spotted him in the market and pulled out a piece of paper. "Mr. Picasso," she said excitedly, "I'm a big fan. Please, could you do a little drawing for me?" Picasso happily complied and quickly etched out a piece of art for her on the paper provided. He smiled as he handed it back to her, and said, "That will be a million dollars." "But Mr. Picasso," the flustered woman replied, "it only took you 30 seconds to do this little masterpiece." "My good woman," Picasso laughed, "it took me 30 years to do that masterpiece in 30 seconds."

Focus plus daily improvement plus time equals genius. Understand that formula deeply and your life will never be the same.

Know what you can excel at—your genius. Discover your talents and then work like crazy to polish them. One of the most important of all personal leadership skills is self-awareness. Know what you are really great at. Reflect on those abilities that others admire in you. Think about those capabilities that just come easily to you—and that flow effortlessly from you. You might be a fantastic communicator or have a way with people. You might possess an extraordinary ability to execute and get things done. Perhaps your special talent lies in innovation and creativity and seeing what everyone else sees but thinking a different thought. Find your genius points and then develop them. Focus plus daily improvement plus time. Start today and in three to five years people will be writing about you. Calling you a genius. Celebrating your magnificence. And don't worry—I'll be one of them.

17

Listen Twice as Much as You Speak

My mom is a very wise woman. As a kid, I loved to talk (still do). In school, I always did well academically but my report cards never failed to note my passion for vigorously exercising my vocal chords on a near-constant basis. One day Mom sat me down and said: "Robin, you were given two ears and one mouth for a reason: to listen twice as much as you speak." Brilliant point (still working on it though).

Listening intently to someone is one of the best ways I know of to honor that person and forge a deep human connection. When you listen to someone—not just with your mind but with every fiber of your being—it sends them a message: "I value what you have to say, and I'm humble enough to listen to your words." So few of us are really good at listening. I'll sit down next to someone on an airplane, at the start of a six-hour flight, and they'll still be talking by the time we land—without having even asked me my name or where I'm from or what I do or the books I've read. Tells me not only that they lack what scientists call "sensory acuity" (an ability to pay attention to the cues around them) but that they were probably not given much listening as kids. Most people's idea of listening is waiting until the other person has finished speaking before answering. And the sad fact is that while one person is talking, most of us are rehearsing our replies.

Listening **intently** to someone is one of the best ways I know of to honor that person and forge a **deep** human connection.

New York attorney general Eliot Spitzer has a line that I love: "Never talk when you can nod." Your effectiveness as a businessperson, as a family member and as a human being will absolutely soar if you get this one right. Listen twice as much as you speak. Become a world-class listener. Get wildly interested in what others have to say to you. And just watch how people respond. They'll fall in love with you. Quickly.

18

Your Customers Buy
with Their Hearts

I'm standing in line at a Starbucks. The Dave Matthews Band is playing in the background. The smell of coffee fills the air. The espresso machines blast away. People are reading, relaxing and talking. The vibe is good. I feel happy here. Feels like home. If you're in business, one of the most important things I suggest that you consider is the idea that people don't buy with their heads so much as with their hearts. The competition in today's marketplace is not for customers' money. Not at all. The only real competition is for their emotions. Touch the hearts of the people you serve and they'll be back for more. Engage their emotions and they'll become your raving fans. Miss this insight and you just might lose your business.

Sure I could spend less on a cup of java. Sure there's a coffee shop closer to where I work. But I love the way going into a Starbucks makes me feel. Relaxed. Happy. Good. And each of us craves good feelings as we live out our days. In so many ways, adults are nothing more than children in grown-up bodies— and children are all about feeling good. On this point about emotions driving customer behavior, Kevin Roberts, CEO of Saatchi & Saatchi, writes, in his superb book *Lovemarks: The Future Beyond Brands*: "In my 35 years in business I have always trusted my emotions. I have always believed that by touching emotion you get the best people to work with you, the best clients to inspire you, the best partners and most devoted customers." Roberts then quotes neurologist Donald Calne: "The essential difference between emotion and reason is that emotion leads to action while reason leads to conclusions." A breathtakingly important point. Human beings move when their emotions are moved.

Human beings move when their emotions are moved.

How does carrying an iPod around make you feel? How does shopping at a hip shop make you feel? How does walking into your favorite restaurant and being greeted like Diddy or Madonna or Bill Clinton make you feel? You get my point. People go where they are made to feel cared for, special and good. People buy from a place of emotional engagement. Seems so obvious. Yet most businesses don't get it.

Here's my bold statement for today: Business is in so many ways about love. Think about it. Success comes by treating your customers with love. Acclaim comes by doing your job with love. Market leadership comes with selling your wares with love. If your customers only like you, you are vulnerable to losing them when a competitor with a cheaper product or a more economical service comes along. Why? Because you've failed to emotionally connect with them. But when your customers love you—because you've touched their hearts by the way that you occur in their lives—you become part of their extended family. You're now a part of their community. They become loyal. They tell the rest of the family about you. And they'll take good care of you should times get tough.

So I'll keep going to Starbucks. I love the place. And if you ever want to find me, I'll be the guy tucked away in the quiet corner, sipping on a grande soy latte with a smile on my face and joy in my heart—feeling the love.

19

Learn to Say No

Every time you say yes to something that is unimportant, you are saying no to something that is important. "Yes men" and "yes women" never create anything great. There's huge value in getting good at saying no.

Say no to the friend who wants to meet over coffee to gossip. Say no to the co-worker who wants to spread his negativity and cynicism. Say no to the relative who laughs at your dreams and makes you doubt yourself. Say no to the social obligations that drain time from your life's work.

Every time you say yes to something that is unimportant, you say no to something that is important.

You can't be all things to all people. The best among us get that. Know your priorities. Know your goals. Know what needs to get done over the coming weeks, months and years for you to feel that you played your best game as a human being. And then say no to everything else. Sure some people around you might not be happy. But would you rather live your life according to the approval of others or aligned with your truth and your dreams?

20

Burn Your Boats

Powerful thought: Great achievement often happens when our backs are up against the wall. Pressure can actually enhance your performance. Your power most fully exerts itself when the heat is on. Who you truly are surfaces only when you place yourself in a position of discomfort and you begin to feel like you're out on the skinny branch. Challenge serves beautifully to introduce you to your best—and most brilliant—self. Please stop and think about that idea for a second or two. Easy times don't make you better. They make you slower and more complacent and sleepy. Staying in the safety zone—and coasting through life—never made anyone bigger. Sure it's very human to take the path of least resistance. And I'd agree it's pretty normal to want to avoid putting stress on yourself by intensely challenging yourself to shine. But greatness never came to anyone normal. (Mahatma Gandhi, Bill Gates, Oprah Winfrey, Mother Teresa, Albert Schweitzer, Andy Grove and Thomas Edison definitely marched to a different drumbeat—thank God).

I've never forgotten the story of the famed explorer Hernando Cortés. He landed on the shores of Veracruz, Mexico, in 1519. Wanted his army to conquer the land for Spain. Faced an uphill battle: an aggressive enemy, brutal disease and scarce resources. As they marched inland to do battle, Cortés ordered one of his lieutenants back to the beach with a single instruction: "Burn our boats." My kind of guy.

Challenge serves beautifully to introduce you to your best—and most brilliant–self.

How fully would you show up each day—at work and in life—if retreat just wasn't an option? How high would you reach, how greatly would you dare, how hard would you work and how loud would you live if you knew "your boats were burning," that failure just wasn't a possibility? Diamonds get formed through intense pressure. And remarkable human beings get formed by living from a frame of reference that tells them they just have to win.

21

Grow Leaders Fast

One of the training programs that we offer companies to help them get to world class in their marketspace is called *Grow The Leader*. Organizations all around the world including NASA and pharmaceutical giant Wyeth are using our unique process to increase employee engagement, enhance culture, dramatically boost performance and produce superior business results. *Grow The Leader* is based on a simple yet powerful concept: The ultimate competitive advantage of your enterprise comes down to a single imperative—your ability to grow and develop leaders faster than your competition. The more quickly you can get every single person in the company demonstrating leadership behavior—regardless of their position—the more quickly you will lead the field. Your race is to grow leaders fast and develop a "culture of leadership" before your competition does.

A leadership culture is one where everyone thinks like an owner, like a CEO or managing director. It's one where *everyone* is entrepreneurial and proactive. This means they focus on getting to solutions rather than on the problems. This means they do whatever it takes to keep customers happy. This means they worry about sales and do their part to reduce costs. This means they take personal responsibility for achieving results that move the business forward (whether they run the mailroom or sit in a boardroom). This means they shape culture, stay positive and lead by example. We've helped our clients create leadership cultures and the results have been nothing short of remarkable.

The ultimate competitive advantage of your enterprise comes down to a single imperative—your ability to grow and develop leaders faster than your competition.

I pray that I've been clear: I'm not saying everyone needs to do the job of a CEO or managing director. Showing leadership doesn't mean every employee will run the organization. That would lead to chaos. Businesses do need someone to set the vision and then lead the team to it. All I'm suggesting is that all the people on your team need to know their role and then show up fully in that role—like a leader would. And when they do—when they think, feel and act like leaders—good things will happen. And soon, your organization will get to great.

22

Your Four-Minute Mile

The philosopher Arthur Schopenhauer once observed: "Most people take the limits of their vision to be the limits of the world. A few do not. Join them." Profound point. The life that you see this very moment isn't necessarily the life of your future. You might be viewing things through the eyes of your fears, limitations and false assumptions. Once you clean up the stained glass window you see the world through, guess what? A whole new set of possibilities appears. Remember, we see the world not as it is but as we are. That idea changed my life, over a decade ago, when I was an unhappy lawyer searching for a better way to live.

Before 1954, it was believed that no runner could ever break the four-minute mile barrier. But after Roger Bannister broke it, many more replicated his feat—within weeks. Why? Because he showed people what was possible. They got a new reference point. And then armed with that belief, people did the impossible.

What's *your* four-minute mile? What bill of goods have you sold yourself as to what's impossible? What false assumptions are you making in terms of what you cannot have, do and be? Your thinking creates your reality. Your beliefs truly become self-fulfilling prophecies (because your beliefs drive your actions—and you will never act in a way that is misaligned with your thinking; the size of your life reflects the size of your thinking). If you think something cannot occur in your life, then there's no way you will take the action required to make that goal a reality. Your "impossibility thinking" manifests itself. Your perceived limitations become the chains that keep you from the greatness you were meant to be. And you are *so* much better than that. Celebrated neurosurgeon Ben Carson expressed it so well when he said: "There is no such thing as an average human being; if you have a normal brain, you are superior."

If you **think** something cannot occur in your life, then there's no way you will take the action required to make that goal a **reality**. Your "impossibility thinking" manifests itself.

23

Push the Envelope

How big do you dream? How fast do you move? How relentlessly do you innovate? I think of Apple on the subject of innovation and their devotion to offering the world "insanely great" products. I just bought my daughter an iPod. She was extraordinarily persistent in her asking—smart kid. Such an array of iPods to select from: the Shuffle, the incredibly sleek Nano, the U2 version of the iPod. Rather than resting on its laurels with the massive success of this product, Apple just keeps innovating, reaching for something even better.

I did a speech for the Young Presidents' Organization the other night. Talked about leadership and how the best get better. Shared how companies can achieve stunning success by making a few simple changes and course corrections. One young entrepreneur came up to me for a chat. I asked him for the best idea he's learned for winning. "Always be pushing the envelope," he replied.

Sure being a leader (at work or at home or in your community) is a lonely act. The very definition of being a leader means you are out in front—with no one else. Taking the road less traveled. Taking responsibility for results in a world that loves to blame and deny responsibility. Seeing possibilities that no one else has yet dreamed of. Challenging the way things are. If you were in the herd, thinking and behaving like everyone else, then you wouldn't be a leader—you'd be a follower. And that's no fun.

Remember, every great leader (or visionary or brave thinker) was initially laughed at. Now they are revered.

So push the envelope. Refuse to accept anything remotely close to mediocrity. Let go of the chains that have bound you to the ordinary. And definitely leave the crowd. The only place you'll reach if you follow the crowd is the exit. Stand for your best. Commit to excellence. Become massively innovative and wear your passion on your sleeve. They might call you different or weird or even crazy. But please remember, every great leader (or visionary or brave thinker) was initially laughed at. Now they are revered.

24

On Obituaries and the Meaning of Life

I'm 41 years old. So I'm at half-time. Assuming I live until I'm 80 (and that's a big assumption because I've learned that the only thing you can expect in life is the unexpected), I'm half way home—half way through the adventure I call my life. I've become more philosophical these days. I'm less willing to waste my time. Less willing to listen to negative people. Less willing to miss an opportunity to be loving, champion another human being, get closer to my dreams, or have some genuine fun. I've also started reading obituaries.

When I read of the lives others have lived, I'm offered clues on what's most important in life. Obituaries of lives well lived actually share consistent themes, I've discovered. Family. Friendships. Contribution to community. The need to take calculated risks. Kindness through small, simple acts. And love. I've yet to read an obituary that says, "he died peacefully in his sleep surrounded by his lawyer, his stockbroker and his accountant." No, the great ones all speak of being close to loved ones and of the impact the deceased had on the world around them.

To lead a beautiful life, I suggest that you need to ask the kinds of questions that will provoke you to think deeply and connect with what matters most. One of the dominant traits of so many of the extraordinary people I've worked with as a success coach is the discipline of being more reflective than most of us. So ask profound questions. Good questions lead to excellent answers and greater clarity. And greater clarity is the DNA of authentic success and personal greatness.

I've yet to read an obituary that says, "he died peacefully in his sleep surrounded by his lawyer, his stockbroker and his accountant."

Here are five big questions that I hope will cause you to go deep and become more philosophical about what truly counts in your life. Most people don't discover how to live until it's time to die. But by then it's too late. Ask yourself these five questions today. Write your answers in your journal. Talk about them. Think about them. Imagine that today is the last day of your life and you are lying on your deathbed. Then ask yourself:

Did I dream richly?
Did I live fully?
Did I learn to let go?
Did I love well?
Did I tread lightly on the earth and leave it better than I found it?

My hope is that the answers you arrive at will help you live with more authenticity, passion and joy. Clarity really does precede success. You can't hit a target you can't even see. And we're really not here that long, when you think about it. We'll all be dust before you know it. So live your potential now. The Chinese say it so well: "The best time to plant a tree was 20 years ago. But the second best time is today."

25

Leadership Isn't a Popularity Contest

Here's an idea that just might transform your entire career (and your life): Being a leader (and in my mind, every single one of us has an obligation to show leadership daily—regardless of title or position) isn't about being liked. It's about doing what's right. So many leaders are afraid of conflict—they have a deep-seated need to be popular and cherished. They hate ruffling feathers and making waves. They are insecure and not so comfortable living in their own skin. But great leaders are different. They fearlessly make tough calls. They speak their truth. They run their own race, making the right decisions and worrying little about public opinion. They are courage in action.

I speak and write a lot about being caring and respectful of people. Treat your people well and they'll treat your customers well. That's a no-brainer. Help people get to their goals and they'll happily help you get to yours. I'll take that value to my grave. See the best in people and be the most compassionate person you know. But being kind doesn't mean being weak.

Being a good human doesn't mean that you don't need to be strong and courageous when required by the circumstances. Not once have I ever suggested that. Extraordinary leadership is a balance between being tender yet tough, compassionate yet courageous, part saint and part warrior, friendly yet firm. (By the way, to help you get to world class professionally and personally, I've recorded an idea-rich and exceptionally practical audio program called "Extraordinary Leadership" which contains my best ideas on the topic. As my gift to you, you can download the presentation for free at robinsharma.com).

All that the best leaders really care about is being fair, doing what's right and getting results. And that brings me to my gentle suggestion to you: Do the right thing rather than doing the popular thing. The best thing to do is generally the hardest thing to do. Please remember that. Make the tough decisions. Speak with candor. Let underperformers know when they are underperforming. Tell your superstars how much you love them. Just be real.

Being a **leader** isn't about being liked. It's about doing what's **right**.

When you lead from a position of truth, justice, fairness and excellence, you'll have your critics. Who cares? I've never seen a critic show up at a deathbed. My friend Dan Sheehan, who runs a great company called WinPlus out of Los Angeles that we've done leadership development work with, once shared this with me: "Great people build monuments from the stones that their critics throw at them." Nice point. Smart guy. If I had listened to all my critics, I'd still be an unhappy lawyer locked to a desk. Thank God I didn't.

26

What Do You Evangelize?

Being an "evangelist" has negative connotations in the world we reside in. But an evangelist, by definition, is simply someone who spreads good news. It's someone who gets stuck on a big idea or a passionate cause and then walks out into his day and spreads the message like a virus. It's someone who gets so engaged in doing something important that it's all he thinks about, dreams about, talks about. It's a human being who understands—at a cellular level—what Dr. Martin Luther King Jr. meant when he said: "If you have not discovered something you are willing to die for, then you are not fit to live." This troubled and uncertain world of ours needs more evangelists: human beings doing great things, blessing lives by their actions, making a difference.

Where did most people's passion for greatness go? Each of us had it as kids. We wanted to be superheroes, astronauts, poets and painters. We wanted to change the world, stand on mountaintops and eat lots of ice cream. Then, as we aged, life began to do its work on us. Fearful people snickered at our dreams. Disappointments began to show up. Life began to hurt us and we began to buy into the propaganda that says we should not think too big, reach too high and love too much. Breaks my heart to think about it. But that's exactly what happens.

You are meant to shine. I believe that fiercely. You are here to find that cause, that main aim, that vital destiny that will move you at the most visceral level and get you up at the crack of dawn with fire in your belly. You are meant to find something that your life will stand for that will consume you, something so beautiful and meaningful that you'd be willing to take a bullet for it. It might mean developing people at work and helping them live their highest potential. It might mean being an innovator who adds outrageous value to your clients and brings cool products to the world. Your cause might involve elevating communities or helping people in need. I recently read about a lawyer who said he was so passionate about being of service to a group of victims he was representing that he wouldn't give up until there was blood coming out of his eyes. Extreme? Maybe. An evangelist? Definitely.

You are here to find that cause, that main aim, that vital destiny that will move you at the most visceral level and get you up at the crack of dawn with fire in your belly.

I'm an evangelist. Talk to anyone who knows me and they'll tell you that my oxygen is helping human beings lead without title and getting organizations to world-class. Sure I have my down times and hard days—find me someone who doesn't. But mostly you'll find me full of enthusiasm, high energy and delight at spreading my message. Am I more special than you? Absolutely not. I've just found my Cause.

I don't know what your life's Most Important To Do is. That's for you to figure out (through some deep reflection, introspection and soul-searching; doing that within a journal is a wise idea). But I do know this: When you find the mission that your life will be dedicated to, you'll wake up each day with that fire in your belly I mentioned. You won't want to sleep. You'll be willing to move mountains to make it happen. You'll find that sense of internal fulfillment that may now be missing from your life. And you'll preach that message to anyone who'll listen. You'll become an evangelist.

27

Under the Kimono: My Best Practices

I just want to help you shine. All I really care about is doing my part to help you get to your greatness. To help you reach your best at work. To help you find happiness at home. To help you make your mark. What's my payoff? Well, when I help you live your finest life, I get to feel significant. I get to feel that I'm making a difference in the world. That I matter. That I'm not walking the planet in vain. That's where so much of my happiness comes from. Truly.

So here's what I thought about in the shower this morning: What are my best practices? In other words, what are the best things that I do to stay at my very best—on game and in potential? Here's what I came up with:

- *Up at 5 a.m. five times a week with naps on the weekends.*
- *A 60-minute "holy hour" once I'm up, for self-development and personal reflection.*
- *five big-time workouts a week.*
- *A 90-minute massage every seven days.*

- *A world-class diet. (But I eat one to two desserts every week—life isn't meant to be too strict; and if I ever see "flourless chocolate cake" on a menu, I order it.)*
- *A period of journaling most days. Journaling builds self-awareness. I also use my journal to write daily goals, plan and record what I'm grateful for, and capture and process new ideas along with lessons learned.*
- *A period of reading each day (from* Harvard Business Review *to* Travel and Leisure *to* Dwell *and good books).*
- *Affirmations or what I call Success Statements throughout the day— especially in the shower. These keep my thoughts locked on what's most important—and thoughts are the ancestors of actions. Right thinking drives right action.*
- *A weekly planning session. I also review my goals here. Usually I do it Sunday morning.*
- *At least one conversation with an interesting person each week to keep my passion high and to surround myself with big ideas. A single conversation can change your life. In an issue of* Business 2.0, *management consultant Jim Collins revealed that one idea, shared in 30 seconds by a mentor, transformed him.*

This very day can be the first day of your new life. It's all your choice.

I have more but these are my best personal practices, the ones that bring out my highest. Pick the ones that resonate with you. Discard the ones that you disagree with. Just find what works for the way you live. Then act on them today. This very day can be the first day of your new life. It's all your choice.

28

Culture Is King

At a leadership training program I recently gave for a group of high-tech managers, a distinguished-looking man came up to me at the break and shared: "I love what you said about the need for each one of us to develop a leadership culture within our organizations. At our company, one of our top priorities is to work on our culture. We talk about it all the time. Last year, our company grew 600%. Our focus on culture-building worked splendidly." Impressive.

As I've suggested earlier, one of your most sustainable competitive advantages will be developing a Culture of Leadership. When clients engage Sharma Leadership International for organizational development and employee training, one of the first areas we focus on is developing the company's culture—because all performance is driven by the culture. Your competitors will copy your products if they are good. They will copy your services. They will copy your branding. But they will never be able to copy your culture. And your culture is the very thing that makes your organization special. Your organization's culture is what sets—and then drives—the standards of behavior. Your culture tells your people what's acceptable and important. Your culture lets people know what your organization values (e.g., honesty, innovation, unending improvement, wowing customers, collaboration, candor and so on). Your organization's culture states its philosophy, its mythology, its religion. To me, culture is king.

One of your most sustainable competitive advantages will be developing what I call a Culture of Leadership.

The five best ways to build culture are as follows:

RITUALS. *I like the "cult" in culture. The best companies, like Dell and Google and Southwest Airlines and Apple and Wal-Mart, have something in common with cults. They have unique rituals like 7 a.m. team huddles or Friday afternoon pizza parties to promote team bonding. Rituals shape culture and keep it special.*

CELEBRATION. *John Abele, founder of the multi-billion-dollar Boston Scientific, once told me over dinner that "you get what you celebrate." Powerful idea. When you see someone living the values your culture stands for, make them a public hero. Behavior that gets rewarded is behavior that gets repeated. Catch people doing good.*

CONVERSATION. *Your people become what the leaders talk about; to get your vision and values into your people's hearts, you need to be talking about that stuff constantly—at employee gatherings, at your weekly meetings, during your daily huddles and at the water cooler. You need to evangelize what you stand for constantly. In his excellent book*

Winning, *Jack Welch said that he spent so much time evangelizing GE's mission that he could call his people at three in the morning and—half asleep—they could re-state it. (He never did.)*

TRAINING. *A mission-critical focus to build culture is employee development. If you agree that your organization's number-one resource is your people, then it only makes sense to invest significantly in developing your number-one resource. Hold seminars and have leadership workshops to instill the values you seek to nurture and build a leadership culture into their hearts and minds. When your people improve, your company will improve.*

STORYTELLING. *Great companies have cultures where great stories are told from generation to generation. The story about how the company was founded in a basement or the story about how a teammate went the extra mile and delivered a customer's baby or the story about how the organization fought back to victory from the brink of disaster. Storytelling cements a company's most closely cherished ideals into the hearts of its people.*

People want to go to work each day and feel they are a part of a community. One of the deepest psychological needs of a human being is the need for belonging. We also want to work for an organization that values us, that promotes our personal growth and that makes us feel that we are contributing to a dream. Get these things right by creating a Culture of Leadership and you'll keep your stars and attract other ones. And wouldn't that be perfect?

29

Your Schedule Doesn't Lie

There's an old phrase that says "what you're doing speaks so loudly I cannot hear what you are saying." You can say that your primary value involves putting your family first, but if time with your family is not all over your schedule, well then the *truth* of the matter is that your family life isn't your priority. You can say that being in world-class physical condition is another top value but if I don't see five or six workouts etched into your weekly schedule, then the reality to be confronted is that your health just isn't as important as you profess it to be. You can argue that self-development is an essential pursuit to you because the better you are, the more effective you'll be. Show me your schedule and I'll discover the truth. Because your schedule doesn't lie.

There can be no authentic success and lasting happiness if your daily schedule is misaligned with your deepest values. That's a big idea that has been so helpful to so many of the executive clients that I coach. If there is a gap between what you do and who you are, you are out of integrity. I call it The Integrity Gap. The greater the chasm between your daily commitments and your deepest values, the less your life will work (and the less happiness you will feel). Why? Because you are not walking your talk. Because your video is not congruent with your audio.

Because you are committing the crime of self-betrayal. Worst crime of all. And the witness that lives within the deepest part of you—your conscience—sees it.

Your schedule is the best barometer for what you truly value and believe to be important.

Your schedule is the best barometer for what you truly value and believe to be important. Too many people talk a good talk. But talk is cheap. Less talk and more do. Show me your schedule and I'll show you what your priorities are. I used to be a litigation lawyer. Witnesses in the courtroom could say what they wanted to. But the evidence never lied.

30

Shine as a Parent

I've had coaching clients fly their private jets to the small airport near our office in Toronto and show up at our first meeting saying something like: "Robin, I have all the money I'll ever need and a bunch of homes scattered around the world along with a ton of public acclaim. But I'm desperately unhappy." I ask why. "Because I lost my family while I built my business. My wife left me and my kids don't even know me . . . that breaks my heart," is how the reply usually goes.

Put your family, along with your health, at the top of your priority list. Family matters. What's the point of getting to your dreams but being alone? And few things are more important than being an extraordinary parent. Kids grow up unbelievably fast. Blink and they're gone—living lives of their own. It seems like only a year or two ago that I witnessed my daughter's birth. Now she's 9 and spends much of her free time playing with her best friend Max (a cocker spaniel desperately in need of some training). It seems like yesterday my son was in a stroller with the chubby cheeks of a baby and the sounds of an infant. Now he's 11, reading even more voraciously than I do and sharing his vision for his future (he wants to be a venture capitalist). Sure it's a little sad watching your children grow up so quickly.

I guess all I can do is stay devoted to them and be generous with my time (my children have always been my number-one priority). Here are some ideas for you to shine in the incredibly important role of parent:

Try not to teach your fears to your kids. Introduce your children to what's possible.

LEAD BY EXAMPLE. *The best way to influence your kids is to walk the talk. Model the behavior you wish to see. Don't preach the beauty of books and learning and then head into your family room to watch three hours of MTV. Those little eyes watch everything you do. I talk about this in* Family Wisdom from the Monk Who Sold His Ferrari, *which is a book that will be very helpful to you as you grow young leaders at home.*

DEVELOP YOUR CHILDREN. *See yourself not just as a parent to your children but as a "developer" of them. It's important to actively develop their minds, hearts and souls. That's your job. Expose them to great art. Take them to interesting restaurants. Introduce them to cool people who produce unique ideas. JFK's father would invite fabulously interesting people to dinner often. During the meal, the Kennedy kids would learn from the guest—and then quiz the visitor to deepen their learning. Smart practice.*

INSPIRE YOUR KIDS. *Big idea: Parents teach their children how to view the world. Parents show kids the way the world works. And* *if you see the world as a place of limitation, so will those little people you are raising. Try not to teach your fears to your kids. Introduce your children to what's possible. Inspire them to be great human beings who will elevate the world—in their own special way. Be an enabler.*

Here's a tool for you that comes from my home. Each night before my kids go to sleep, I make four statements to them. "You can do whatever you want to do when you grow up." "Never give up." "Whatever you do, do it well." And "Remember how much your dad loves you." Been doing that every night for four years. They often say, "Dad, we know all this stuff now. We know we should never give up and how much you love us. It's getting boring." But I have a sense that one day, perhaps when I'm old and wrinkled, a letter will come in the mail from Colby or Bianca, my two favorite people on the planet. And on that piece of paper will be simple words saying, "Dad, I'm living a great life. Thank you for being the father you were. And thank you for those four statements each night. They made a difference."

31

Be a Merchant of Wow

Just checked into the Hotel Victor here on South Beach before I wrote this chapter. I saw it being renovated a few months ago and made a mental note to check it out on my next visit to Miami. So here I am, waiting to be impressed, just aching for a reason to tell you something good about this place in a world where so many businesses are boring, slow and stale.

I like trying new hotels when I travel. I observe what to do (and mostly what not to do) when it comes to customer service, study cool design (which stimulates big ideas I can then hand over to my team for our products, ranging from CD covers to clothing) and check out whether the hotel understands that in this "experience economy" we now live in, the customers must be taken on a journey from start to finish that makes them go "wow."

Good news! This place is amazing. Big smile when I entered from the doorman and a warm greeting. Ultra-cool design inside (none of the stark white of SOBE that used to be so hip that everyone copied it—which then made it un-hip). Lots of green and fresh colors. Sexy music and vibe. Super nice front desk staff—the smile thing again with a wonderful offer of Evian water with a slice of lime while I was checking in. And since the MTV Video Music Awards are shooting a video with The Killers tonight down by the pool, Karin asked me whether I wanted a room that would allow me to watch all the action. Sure—I don't need much sleep anyway.

Eric the bellman showed me the workout facility and then the spa. Best hotel gym I've seen since the Sanderson in London. And the room is awesome—art deco, impeccably clean and stylishly put together. All very impressive. Stunning, actually—which is the standard I encourage you to aspire to.

In this "experience economy" we now live in, the customers must be taken on a journey from start to finish that makes them go "WOW."

Hotel Victor under-promised and then over-delivered. It had a chance to win me over, and through well-trained staff, unique and superbly kept facilities and excellent amenities, it did. Now I'm going back downstairs to try its food (everyone raves about its restaurant, where the chef has a spice rack of 1000 spices that he uses in his cooking). I bet I'll be wowed.

32

Getting What You Want While Loving What You Have

Some pundits encourage us to enjoy the moment and appreciate what we have, suggesting that constantly striving for more is unhealthy and the primary source of our discontent. And others say that, as human beings, we were built to push beyond our comfort zones each day and reach for something higher—to become great. I've struggled a lot with this issue, as I articulate a personal philosophy that I will live my life under. I think I've found the answer, a solution that feels right to me: It's a *balance*, I've realized. I call it The Mandela Balance.

Nelson Mandela, a man I greatly admire, once said: "After climbing a great hill, one finds that there are many more hills to climb. I have taken a moment here to rest, to steal a view of the glorious vista that surrounds me, to look back on the distance I have come. But I can only rest for a moment, for with freedom comes responsibilities, and I dare not linger, for my long walk has not yet ended."

To me, Nelson Mandela is suggesting that it truly is all about a balance. Enjoy the view from where you are at. Savor how far you have come. Be grateful for where you are along the journey that is your life. Live in the moment. But also remember that with the gifts that reside within you come great responsibilities. I believe that every human being has a "duty to shine." We must not rest on our past wins and become complacent. We must walk out into the world—each day—and do our best to be of greater service to others, realize more of our potential and become better citizens on the planet. We must continually walk toward our fears and make more of our lives. We must constantly play a bigger game and use our creative talents to do, be and see more. This drive to realize more of our greatest selves has, I believe, been knitted into our DNA and to deny it is to deny our human nature.

This world was built by people who felt some discontent with the way things were and knew they could do better.

And yes, as we set higher dreams and raise our personal standards, we will create some discontent. But this world was built by people who felt some discontent with the way things were and knew they could do better. "Show me a completely contented person and I'll show you a failure," observed Thomas Edison. Politically incorrect these days, I know. But I think he was speaking truth. The greatest among us were not satisfied with the way things were. Think Gandhi. Think Mother Teresa. Think Archbishop Desmond Tutu. Think Bill Gates. Think Einstein. Think Mandela.

So love what you have. And then go for what you want. Enjoy the climb up the mountain. But never take your eyes off the summit.

33

Think like a CEO

I spoke to the leadership team of Satyam Computer Services a few months ago. Amazing company. One of Asia's fastest growing IT firms: zero to $1 billion in less than 10 years. 23,000 employees. The chairman is a visionary. I'll share one of his powerful ideas. There are 1500 top managers at Satyam. They run 1500 different divisions and functions. So he tells them that they are not really managers—they are the CEOs of their own small businesses. The larger corporation is simply an "investor" that they need to keep happy. It provides them with resources, structures and opportunities. They just have to return results. The concept inspires them to take ownership of their functional areas and behave like entrepreneurs. It gets them to act like real leaders. It encourages them to be part of the solution rather than part of the problem. Brilliant.

Take personal **responsibility** for the success of your business. Show up like an entrepreneur. Grow sales. Cut costs. Get **good** stuff done.

You are the CEO of your functional area. Do you have a finance function at your company? You are the CEO of that area, that small business. Work in human resources? That's your small business. Clean-up at the end of the day? You run a clean-up business that serves the larger company you work with. Take personal responsibility for the success of your business. Show up like an entrepreneur. Grow sales. Cut costs. Get good stuff done. You will shine in your career. And the CEO will love you.

34

Act like an Athlete

One of the best ways I know to create spectacular results in the most important areas of your life is through daily practice. Top athletes know that practice is how you get to greatness. I was in Moscow a while back for a series of speeches and workshops. One morning I went down to the hotel gym for a workout. It was 6 a.m. Guess who was there? Mary Pierce, the tennis star. For two hours, she ran, lifted weights, did sit-ups and countless push-ups. She was paying the price for success.

You need to practice to get to your greatness. Athletes know this so very well. Why does it seem so foreign to the rest of us? Sure practice takes discipline. But as my friend Nido Qubein (the business consultant and motivational speaker) often says: "The price of discipline is always less than the pain of regret." Wise man.

What I'm suggesting is that personal and professional greatness takes work. I would never suggest that you could get to your dreams without having to make some sacrifices and pay the price in terms of dedication and self-control. "Pay the price." Words with the ring of truth. The best among us make it all look so easy. I call it the Swan Effect—elite performers make personal and business mastery look effortless and seem to make things happen as gracefully as a swan moves along the water. But, like the swan, what you don't get to see is all the planning, discipline, hard work and near-flawless execution taking place below the surface.

Top athletes know that practice is how you get to greatness.

In my life, I have a series of practices that set me up for a great day. I've shared those with you. Yes, sometimes life sends you unexpected challenges that knock you off track—that's just life happening. But with a series of best practices in place to keep you at your highest, you'll stay in a positive state much more often. This is a simple yet life-changing idea that has helped so many of our clients. Practices that will lock you into your best state include a morning journaling session where you record your feelings, thoughts and the blessings you are grateful for. Or you may start your day with a strong workout and an elite performer's meal. I often listen to music for 15 minutes, as it not only energizes me, it makes me feel happier. I also use Success Statements or affirmations to get my mind focused. Success and joy and inner peace don't just show up. You need to create them. Find your series of practices, perform them with consistency. And then go out into this beautiful world of ours and shine.

35

Be Wildly Enthusiastic

"Be enthusiastic" smacks of the obvious. "Be energetic" sounds trite. "Be passionate" seems boring. Yet without enthusiasm, energy and passion, you cannot lead your field and an organization cannot get to world class. (Hey, I never suggested this leadership stuff was rocket science.) Ralph Waldo Emerson once said: "Every great and commanding movement in the annals of the world is due to the triumph of enthusiasm." And Samuel Ullman observed: "Nobody grows old merely by living a number of years. We grow old by deserting our ideals. Years may wrinkle the skin but to give up enthusiasm wrinkles the soul." Enthusiasm matters.

The people I love to be around are generally those that have a simple, heartfelt quality: They are enthusiastic. Wildly so. They are open to life. They are curious. They love to learn. They smile when they see me. And they have a lot of fun. Play hard or don't play at all.

Today, show up at work with all the enthusiasm you can genuinely muster. Be outrageously energetic and madly alive. See the best in people. Go the extra mile to delight your customers. See the opportunity for learning and personal evolution amidst a seeming setback. Embrace change as a chance to grow. Have a laugh with a teammate. Tell your loved ones you adore them. Spread some passion. I'll be the first to agree that you can't control what happens to you each day. But with an abundance of enthusiasm, I have no doubt that whatever the coming hours bring, you will handle them with grace, strength and a smile.

Be outrageously energetic and madly alive.

36

Success Isn't Sexy

Too many leadership experts make being successful and fulfilled sound complicated. They preach the latest technique and offer the latest modality that they say will speed you to your greatest life. Take a magic pill or try the latest fad and all will be fine— life will be perfect.

Nonsense. Yes, crafting an extraordinary existence takes work. Of course, getting to greatness—personally and professionally—requires sacrifices. A primary sign of maturity is the ability to give up instant gratification for a much more spectacular pleasure down the road. And true, the right thing to do is generally the hardest thing to do. But here's the good news: With daily, consistent effort in the direction of your dreams and an application of the fundamentals of success, you really can get to the place you've always dreamed of getting to.

Success isn't sexy. It's all about working the basics of excellence with a passionate consistency. I love that word. Consistency. It's amazing how far you will get by just staying with something long enough. Most people give up too early. Their fears are bigger than their faith, I guess.

Stick to the fundamentals that you know in your heart are true and you'll do just fine. What are those fundamentals?

Things like being positive, taking responsibility for your role in what's not working in your life, treating people well, working hard, being an innovator rather than a follower, getting up early, setting your goals, speaking your truth, being self-disciplined, saving your money, caring for your health and valuing your family. I told you that you already know this stuff. Nike is a client of ours. And they got it right with all that JDI stuff: Just Do It! As I wrote in my book *Who Will Cry When You Die?*, "The smallest of actions is always better than the noblest of intentions."

Don't complicate things. Getting to your best life is simple. Not easy but simple. It just takes focus and effort. That philosophy about the thousand mile journey beginning with a single step is true. Do a little each day to get you to your goals and over time you'll get there. Small daily gains lead to giant results over a lifetime.

It's **amazing** how far you will get by just staying with something long enough. Most people give up too early. Their fears are bigger than their **faith**.

Big idea: Personal—and organizational—greatness is not about revolution but about evolution, those small but consistent wins. Sam Walton began with a single store. Richard Branson began with his first little record shop. Steve Jobs started Apple out of his garage. Hey, I started with a few cases of self-published books that I'd printed in a Kinko's copy shop. And only 23 people showed up for my first seminar—21 of them were family members. Every dream starts small. But you need to start. Today.

37

On Cuddle Parties and the Sad State of the World

Get this: I just heard that people across North America are showing up at designated places to have "cuddle parties." Strangers get together, introduce themselves and then spend time cuddling. Nothing more—just feeling the touch of another human being and feeling connected. Hmmm.

The paradox of our wired world is that as we become more **connected** electronically, we become less connected **emotionally**.

The paradox of our wired world is that as we become more connected electronically, we become less connected emotionally. People spend hours each night reading blogs, down-

loading podcasts and surfing the internet. But they've forge
the importance of old-fashioned conversation. They've neglect
the power of breaking bread with family and friends. And they've
lost sight of the importance of human touch.

Do what you like. I'm not a judge. But I have no plans
to show up at a cuddle party any time soon. I'd rather work to
build the bonds of humanity with those already around me by
being loving to my kids and other family, kind to my friends and
supportive of my teammates and clients. Just doing that would
give me all the cuddles I need.

38

The Value of Good

After I gave a speech for a major telecommunications company, a woman walked up to me with tears in her eyes. "Robin, I've read all your books and try my best to live the kind of life you write about. But there was a man who actually lived your message. He died a few months ago. He was my dad." She paused, and looked down at the floor. "Five thousand people showed up at my father's funeral," she said. "The whole town was there. I was so honored to see that."

"Was your dad a well-known businessperson?" I asked. "No," she replied. "A popular politician?" I wondered aloud. "No," she whispered. "Was your father some kind of a local celebrity?" "No, Robin, he wasn't at all." "Then why did 5000 people come to your dad's funeral?" I had to ask.

Another long pause. "They came because my father was a man who always had a smile on his face. He was the kind of person who was always the first to help someone in need. He always treated people incredibly well and was unfailingly polite. He walked the earth ever so lightly. Five thousand people showed up at my dad's funeral because he was good."

Whatever happened to valuing being good? Reality TV shows exhibit the worst of human behavior. We see music superstars who swear every five seconds. We read about corporate leaders who fill their pockets to buy bigger boats while share-holders lose their life savings. I loved the movie *Wall Street*. But Gordon Gekko got it wrong: Greed isn't good. Good is good.

Some people laugh at the notion of being nice and decent and noble. "That's a sign of weakness," I hear. Nope. It's a sign of strength. Soft is hard. It's easy to put yourself first. It's easy to get angry when someone disagrees with you. It's easy to complain or condemn or take the path of least resistance. What takes guts is to stand for something higher, to behave greater and to be of service to others. Like Mandela. Like Gandhi. Like King. Heroes of mine. I wish I could be one-quarter as good as them.

Gordon Gekko got it wrong: Greed isn't good. **Good** is good.

Sorry for ranting, but this is a big topic for me. I'll be the first to tell you I'm far from perfect. I'm just a messenger—an ordinary man. But I'll tell you one thing—I do my best to be good. That quest keeps me up at night. And I hold myself to a standard far higher than anyone could ever expect from me. Do I always get it right? No. Am I always at peace and without anger? No. Do I always model my message? No. I try to each day but I slip sometimes.

I'm not saying that treating people with respect means you don't hold them to high standards and expect excellence from them. It doesn't mean you don't set boundaries and get tough when you have to. Showing leadership isn't about being liked by all. It's about doing what's right. And what's good.

39

Grace under Pressure

Dr. Martin Luther King Jr. once said in a speech: "The ultimate measure of a man is not where he stands in moments of comfort and convenience, but where he stands at times of challenge and controversy." So true. What we are as human beings presents itself more fully in times of adversity than at times of ease. Anyone can be positive, polite and kind when things are going well. What distinguishes people with an extraordinary character from the rest of us is how they respond when life sends one of its inevitable curves. They don't crumble or surrender. They reach deeply into themselves and present even more of their highest nature to the world.

Just a couple of hours ago, I was on the runway, ready to fly home from London. The flight had been delayed by a few hours so it felt good to be so close to takeoff. I had my iPod in place, a new book to read and my journal. Then, the pilot's voice came over the public address system: "The ground crew has found a metal instrument in one of the tires. We regret that we must cancel this flight." The reactions that statement provoked were fascinating.

One man close to me became belligerent to a flight attendant. A couple in another row grumbled loudly. A businessman in a dark suit actually kicked the seat in front of him. Yet some passengers responded differently, with a quiet humanity. An elderly gentleman smiled as he helped others take their bags down from the overhead compartments. A teenager, rather than trying to rush off the plane like most of the other passengers, stopped to help a woman with a disability. The lady sitting next to me laughed and said, "Hey, it's not the end of the world," before calling her kids and sharing her adventure with them. The wisest among us have a remarkable ability to maintain grounded when times get tough.

No life is perfect; mine certainly isn't. We all must face challenges, both large and small. This very minute, somewhere in the world, there are parents dealing with the death of a child. This very minute, someone has suffered an accident that will devastate their loved ones. This very minute, there are human beings dealing with illness in a hospital bed. Sickness, loss, disappointment. No one gets through life without experiencing this stuff. But you and I have the power to choose to rise above our external circumstances. We always have the choice to be strong and positive when things fall apart. We have the right to use our stumbling blocks as stepping stones to our greatest life. This isn't motivational sloganeering. I believe this is truth.

What distinguishes people with an extraordinary character from the rest of us is how they respond when life sends one of its inevitable curves.

Grace under pressure. That's what separates leaders from followers. It's that beautiful quality that inspires others and reflects a well-developed spirit. It's a trait that allows you to carve out a spectacular life—one you'll be proud of at the end. My seatmate was right—things could have been so much worse. I'm safe. I have my health. I have two wonderful children. I have work I love and so much to be grateful for. Sure I now have to wait a few hours to catch the next flight home. Maybe I'll get started on that book my editor keeps asking me about.

40

To Be More Productive, Relax and Have More Fun

Spending all your time working will not make you more productive. In my experience, and I've been at this for over 10 years, few people get their best ideas at work. I invite you to take a moment to think about that. Checking your email messages on your BlackBerry every 60 seconds will not make you more effective. Burning the candle at both ends doesn't tap into your natural pool of creativity. Refusing to take vacations will not make you a star performer. Here's a big lesson I've learned: I get my best ideas—the thoughts that have really elevated my business and revolutionized my life—when I'm relaxed and having fun.

There's great value in making the time to chill out and do the things that fill your heart with joy. Newton didn't come up with his breakthrough observations on the laws of physics while rushing to catch a subway. Einstein spent a ton of time sailing and connecting with his childlike self. The creator of the sewing machine came up with the idea while dreaming about an island native holding a spear with a hole in the end of it. I came up with the whole concept behind *Leadership Wisdom from the Monk*

Who Sold His Ferrari: The 8 Rituals of Visionary Leaders while taking a long solo drive out in the country. When the idea hit me, I
pulled over onto a dirt road and downloaded the ideas into my
journal for more than two hours. An unforgettable experience
for me.

I get my best ideas—the thoughts that have really elevated my business and revolutionized my life—when I'm relaxed and having fun.

I often joke with my audiences that I make most of my
income on a ski hill. People smile. But they get my point. You
need to make space for your genius to flow. We get our creative
bursts, those idea torrents that take our business and personal
lives to the next level, while we are skiing or drinking coffee
in a Starbucks or walking in the woods or meditating with a
sunrise. Those pursuits are not a waste of time. No way. Those
pursuits are a superb use of your time. Creativity comes when
you are relaxed, happy and enjoying the moment. And when
it comes, it can bring ideas that rock your world. All it takes
is one good idea to get you to previously unimagined results.
Relaxing, taking vacations and making time for fun actually
makes you more successful.

And these pursuits make you money. Mireille Guiliano,
the CEO of Clicquot, said it well: "We have to take 'beach time,'
a space for ourselves every day, because we live in a world of

burnout. Even if you take 20 or 30 minutes for yourself, you'll be a better worker, a better colleague, a better person. It benefits the people around you as much as it benefits you."

Get this: Hewlett-Packard recently noted that constant interruptions of technology actually took 10 points off the IQ of an average employee in a work environment. And the U.S. software firm Veritas saw something amazing happen after it introduced "email-free Fridays": Friday became the most productive and creative day of the week.

So have some fun. Laugh with your co-workers. Go for a walk at lunch. Go fishing or swimming or golfing this weekend. Maybe sit on a beach for a week down in the Caribbean or visit the great museums in France and Italy. Or just take a nap and relax. And if anyone tells you that you're wasting time, you have my permission to say: "But Robin told me I'm being productive." And then go back to sleep.

41

The Two Magic Words

I sometimes get a little bothered by ingratitude. I try to treat people well, help them win and celebrate them, so that they reach for their best life. Sometimes, I'd just love to hear two magic words: "Thank you."

Yes, I know that if you do something good for someone with the expectation of a reward it's not a gift—it's a trade. And I know that good things happen to people who do good things. And I know that life has a very fair accounting system and as one sows, one will reap. But I'd still like to hear those two magic words more often.

I had breakfast with a friend the other day. He's helped so many people in his organization realize their highest potential—as leaders and as humans. He looked at me and said: "Robin, after all these years in business, I can count on one hand the number of people who have told me that they appreciate what I've done for them."

I believe I'm offering you a very real point. According to Gallup research, the number-one reason employees leave their organization is not because they were not being paid enough; they leave because they were not given enough appreciation. Your talent goes to the competition because no one said thank you to them. Max De Pree, the former CEO of Herman Miller, sagely observed: "The first responsibility of a leader is to define reality. The last is to say thank you."

So today, take a moment and think about the people in your life who need to be cherished, appreciated and told that their support has been helpful. Offer a heartfelt and enthusiastic "thank you." Those two magic words don't cost anything. But they will make a world of difference.

> Today, take a moment and think about the **people** in your life who need to be **cherished**, appreciated and told that their support has been helpful.

42

The Value of Dying Daily

I have no desire to be the richest person in the graveyard. To me, a life well lived is mostly about being surrounded by people I love, staying healthy and happy (no one's happy all the time, except in the movies, by the way), stepping toward my highest potential each day, doing work I love and having an impact on the world around me. So how can you stay focused on the things that are most important to you amidst the daily pressures of life? Die daily.

I wrote about this in *The Monk Who Sold His Ferrari*, but the point of wisdom bears repeating: Connecting to the fact that life is short and no one knows when it will end is a great personal habit to stay centered on your highest priorities. Waking up each morning and asking yourself, "How would I show up today if this day was my last?" is not some cheesy motivational exercise. It's a profound way to bring some urgency and commitment into your days. Apple CEO Steve Jobs said it far more powerfully than I ever could when he observed: "No one wants to die. Even people who want to go to heaven don't want to die to get there. And yet death is the destination we all share. No one has ever escaped it. And that is as it should be, because death is very likely the single best invention of life."

Most of us let life act on us—we are asleep at the wheel of our own lives. And the days really do slip into weeks, the weeks into months and the months into years. Before we know it, we are lying on our deathbeds, wondering where all the time went. I've talked to a lot of elderly people who express that very sentiment, with tears in their eyes. A participant in a recent seminar made the point beautifully, sharing the following quote from one of his family members with me: "When the sun shone and the shops were invitingly open—alas—I forgot my shopping. Now the night has fallen—and I remember my shopping."

Waking up each morning and asking yourself, "How would I show up today if this day was my **last?**" is not some cheesy motivational exercise. It's a **profound** way to bring some urgency and commitment into your days.

I have a gentle challenge for you: Die daily. Connect with your mortality each morning. Then give yourself over to life. Live like tomorrow will not come. Take some risks. Open your heart a little wider. Speak your truth. Show your respect for the gift of life that's been given to you. Shine brightly today. Chase your dreams. It's tragic that most people would rather cling to security than reach for their best. And then, wake up tomorrow and reach even higher. At the end, people will remember you as one of the great ones. And your funeral will be a celebration.

43

Client-Focused vs. Out to Lunch

It's Saturday morning as I write this chapter. I woke up nice and early to get a great start to this gift of a day. I spent an hour journaling, read and had an excellent conversation with my kids. I then set out to have a workout at the health club I exercise at, which opens at 8 a.m. When I arrived, I saw all these people standing in the parking lot. This particular club has a bridge going over a little river that leads from the parking lot to the main building and tennis courts. Yesterday, we had monsoon-like rains and the bridge collapsed. A few of the employees were checking out the damage.

So I walked up. It was about 7:50 and I was ready for a nice, big workout to energize me for the day. I'm a client, one of the people who keeps them in business. But they didn't seem to get that. No greeting. No smile. No warmth. Just a continued conversation about the destroyed bridge.

I asked whether the club was still open. They laughed. One of the employees said, "We won't be open for a while." Okay . . . a little more information might be helpful, guys. But no more information came. No data on when the club might re-open or a solution for me such as alternative clubs that could allow me to work out for the interim until this place gets up and running again. I turned away, receiving further evidence that this organization just doesn't get it. And that it just doesn't care anymore. It once did.

In the past, it offered excellent service, excellent facilities and excellent amenities. I'd get a birthday card signed by the whole team once a year and they always used my name when I walked in (which felt good even though I knew they'd look up my name when they'd swipe my card as I entered). Then things began to slip. They got successful. Nothing fails like success. Richard Carrion was right. They stopped training their team. They let the machines get old. And so they took us—the clients—for granted. The bridge isn't the only thing broken there.

Business is about **loving** the people who do business with you and giving them more **value** than they have any right to expect.

And guess what? If a new club opens up that shows it understands why it is in business—to add value and delight its customers—I'll be the first to show up. To me, business is about loving the people who do business with you and giving them more value than they have any right to expect. Care for your clients. No . . . astonish them. And your success and sustainability will be guaranteed. Pretty simple idea. So few get it.

44

Lead Without Title

When I go into an organization to help develop and grow leaders, the client often asks me to help employees understand what leadership is all about. Leadership has nothing to do with the title on your business card or the size of your office. Leadership is not about how much money you make or the clothes you wear. Leadership is a philosophy. It's an attitude. It's a state of mind. It's a way of operating. And it's available to each one of us. No matter what you do within an organization. Robert Joss, dean of Stanford Graduate School of Business, made the point splendidly when he observed: "By leadership I mean taking complete responsibility for an organization's well-being and growth, and changing it for the better. Real leadership is not about prestige, power or status. It is about responsibility." The invitation I offer to every group of employees I work with: Lead without title.

Here's an example. I spend a lot of my life on airplanes and traveling so I'm hard on my luggage. The handle on my carry-on luggage broke after my tour of Russia (you have to put a visit to St. Petersburg on your list of places to visit before you die). Anyway, I took the piece in to Evex, a dealer in Toronto. The young man at the counter treated me wonderfully and, within a few days, the handle was fixed. Perfect.

While in New York a little while later, the handle broke again. I assumed that I'd have to pay for the repair when I went back to Evex. Most businesses put clients through so many hurdles: If you haven't saved the receipt you are out of luck. If you don't know who did the initial repair we cannot help. If you didn't buy it at this location you don't exist. Well, Evex is different. They just get it. They understand that without treating their customers well, there is no business. They haven't forgotten who puts food on their table each night. Treat your customers like royalty and you cannot help but win.

When I explained that the handle had broken again, the young woman at the counter—without a moment of hesitation—apologized for the problem I faced. She then said: "We promise you that you will have your carry-on in perfect order within three days. And of course, sir, there will be no charge." No bureaucracy around needing the receipt from the previous repair. No hassles. No issues. Just great service, with a giant smile.

"Real leadership is not about prestige, power or status. It is about responsibility."

This woman showed true leadership. She quickly diagnosed the problem, assumed personal responsibility and made the right decision. Part of the solution versus part of the problem. And she wowed her customer in the process. She wasn't the owner. Not the supervisor. Not a manager. Just a leader without title.

45

Do Your Part

Big question for you: "What are you doing to help build a new and better world?" Don't blame the politicians. Don't blame those around you. Don't blame your parents or your background. Doing so is playing the victim and this world has far too many people playing the victim when they could be sharing their brilliance and making a profound difference. Mother Teresa said it so much better than I ever could: "If each of us would only sweep our own doorstep, the whole world would be clean."

Blaming others is excusing yourself. Telling yourself that you—as an army of one—cannot have an impact is giving away your power. After a hurricane a while ago, a couple of college kids got their hands on empty school buses and drove them into the ravaged area when everybody else said the city was impenetrable. A little man in a loincloth named Mahatma Gandhi freed an entire nation. A woman named Rosa Parks sparked a civil rights movement because she refused to sit at the back of a bus. Ordinary people really can do extraordinary things. I love what Anita Roddick, founder of The Body Shop, once said: "If you think you're too small to have an impact, try going to bed with a mosquito in the room."

Live by what I call the Jennifer Aniston Rule. In an issue of *Vanity Fair,* Aniston said that she gives herself one day to play victim after experiencing a challenging event. After that day of feeling powerless and sorry for herself, she wakes up and takes ownership for the way her life looks. She takes personal responsibility for her part in the problem—even if that only amounted to 1%. That's personal leadership in action. "It doesn't matter who you are, or where you come from. The ability to triumph begins with you. Always," offered entertainment superstar Oprah Winfrey.

Blaming others is excusing yourself. Telling yourself that you—as an army of one—cannot have an impact is giving away your power.

What don't you like about your life or the organization you work for or the country you live in? Make a list. Write it down. Shout it out. And then do something to improve things. Anything. Start small or go big. Just do something. As you exercise your power to choose, guess what? Your power grows. And as you work within your sphere of influence to make things better, guess what? Your sphere of influence expands. So do your part. Today. Now. The world will be better for it.

46

Do You Play?

I dropped off my son, Colby, at his friend's house this past weekend. When his buddy walked up to our car to greet him, I asked: "What are you guys going to do?" The reply came in one big word: "Play." Perfect answer.

Children are our teachers. I'm not the guru in our home—my kids are. As I drove back to my place, I reflected on the importance of play. How often do you ask an adult "What do you plan on doing today?" and get the response "Play"? Maybe that's why our world is broken.

Adults are nothing more than **deteriorated** children.

What would your life look like if there was more play? What would your experience of work be like if you had more fun doing your job, no matter what job you do? What would your relationships look like with more spontaneity, laughter, festivity and youthful—no, wild—abandon? As adults, we stop playing once we assume the responsibilities of life. Adults are nothing more than deteriorated children. Why? It doesn't have to be that way. Make the time to play. Find the time to be a little reckless and silly. Be imaginative at work and bring curiosity back to your days. Get back to that sense of wonder you knew when life was all about make-believe, riding your bike and enjoying every second of this journey called living. And the next time someone looks at you—with your briefcase, business suit and serious face—and asks what you plan on doing today, I invite you to confidently give the only reply that matters: "I'm going out to play."

47

Avoid the "Four F's Syndrome"

Most training and learning doesn't last. No stickiness. We attend a seminar and vow to transform our lives. We say we'll be better parents, more effective leaders and wiser human beings. Two days later, it's back to business as usual—seeing the negative, playing the victim and being cranky. The learning didn't work. Because we didn't change.

No one wants to fail. So most of us don't even try.

Having helped hundreds of thousands of people create *sustained* change, and businesses around the world win in their markets, I've identified four main reasons why people resist change and often don't take the steps to elevate their careers and their lives, even when they have the opportunity to do so. With greater awareness of these four factors—which I call the Four F's Syndrome—you can make better choices. And when you make better choices, you are certain to experience better results. Big idea: Personal leadership begins with self-awareness because you can't improve a weakness or a blind spot you don't even know about. In other words, once you know better you can do better.

Here are the four things that keep us from making the changes we want to make:

FEAR. *People fear leaving their safe harbor of the known and venturing off into the unknown. Human beings crave certainty—even when it limits them. Most of us don't like trying something new—it brings up our discomfort. The key here is to* manage *your fear by doing the very thing that frightens you. That's the best way to destroy a fear. Do it until you're no longer scared. The fears you run away from run toward you. The fears you don't own will own you. But behind every fear wall lives a precious treasure.*

FAILURE. *No one wants to fail. So most of us don't even try. Sad. We don't even take that first step to improve our health or to deepen our working relationships or to realize a dream. In my mind, the only failure in life is the failure to try. And I deeply believe that the greatest risk you can ever take is not taking risks. Take that small step and do it fast. Sports superstar Michael Jordan once said: "There was never any fear for me, no fear of failure. If I miss a shot, so what?" Failure is just an essential part of realizing success. There can be no success without failure.*

FORGETTING. *Sure we leave the seminar room after an inspirational workshop ready to change the world. But then we get to the office the next day and reality sets in. Difficult teammates to deal with. Unhappy customers to satisfy. Demanding bosses to appease. Uncooperative suppliers. No time to act on the commitments we made for personal and professional leadership. So we forget them. Here's a key to success: Keep your commitments top of mind. Heighten your awareness around them. Better awareness—Better choices. Better choices—Better results.*

Keep your self-promises front and center. Don't forget them. Put them on a three-by-five-inch card that you post on your bathroom mirror and read every morning. Seems silly, works beautifully. (You should see my bathroom mirror.) Talk about them a lot (you become what you talk about). Write about them each morning in your journal.

FAITH. *Too many people have no faith. They are cynical. "This leadership training and personal development stuff doesn't work." Or "I'm too old to change." Cynicism stems from disappointment. Cynical and faithless people were not always like that. They were filled with possibilities and hope as kids. But they tried and perhaps failed. And rather than staying in the game, recognizing that failure is the highway to success, they shut down and grew cynical. Their way to avoid getting hurt again.*

So there you go, the four F's of why we resist transformation and showing real leadership within our lives. Understand them and you can then manage and overcome them. Because awareness really does precede success. And ordinary people really can craft extraordinary lives. I see it happen all the time. You truly can get to greatness. Trust me. But you have to start. And how will you know if you don't even try?

48

Problems Reveal Genius

Problems are servants. Problems bring possibilities. They help you grow and lead to better things, both in your organization and within your life. Inside every problem lies a precious opportunity to improve things. Every challenge is nothing more than a chance to make things better. To avoid them is to avoid growth and progress. To resist them is to decline greatness. Embrace and get the best from the challenges in front of you. And understand that the only people with no problems are dead.

An unhappy customer yelling at you might seem like a problem. But to a person thinking like a leader, that scenario is also a giant opportunity to improve the organization's processes to ensure that doesn't happen again and to get some feedback that may be used to enhance products and services. So the problem has actually helped to improve the company. Free market research.

An interpersonal conflict at work can seem like a problem. But if you think like a leader and use the circumstance to build understanding, promote communication and enrich the relationship, the problem has actually made you better. It has been fodder for your growth and served you nicely. Bless it.

An illness or a divorce or the loss of a loved one might seem like a problem. Sure it's painful (been there, done that, on the divorce side). But I've been shaped by my saddest experiences. They've brought me depth, compassion and wisdom. They have given me self-awareness. They've made me the man that I am. I wouldn't trade them for the world.

The only people with no problems are dead.

Problems reveal genius. World-class organizations have a culture that sees problems as opportunities for improvement. Don't condemn them—learn from them and embrace them. World-class human beings turn their wounds into wisdom. They leverage their failures to bring them closer to success. They don't see problems. They see possibilities. And that's what makes them great. Remember, a mistake is only a mistake if you make it twice.

49

Love Your Irritations

The things that drive you crazy are actually giant opportunities. The people who press your buttons are actually your greatest teachers. The issues that make you angry are actually your biggest gifts. Be grateful for them. Love them.

The people or circumstances that take you out of your power have extraordinary value: They reveal your limiting beliefs, fears and false assumptions. The celebrated psychologist Carl Jung once said: "Everything that irritates us about others can lead us to an understanding of ourselves." Powerful point. How much would you pay someone who promised that they could pinpoint exactly what is holding you back from your greatest life? How much would it be worth to get intimate information and intelligence on why you are not exactly at the place where you've always dreamed of being? The things that irritate, annoy and anger you are entry points into your evolution and elevation as a human being. They are signposts for what you need to work on and the fears you need to face. They are gifts of growth. You can blame the people who trigger you and make it all about them. Or you can do the wise thing and look deeply into yourself to discover the reasons for your negative reaction. Use the challenges to grow self-awareness. Because how can you overcome a fear you are not even aware of? And how can you transcend an insecurity you don't even know you have?

As you begin to shed light on your personal weaknesses and take responsibility for them, you actually begin the very process of shedding them. Shadows exposed to the light begin to disappear. You become stronger. More powerful. More of who you were meant to be. You begin to see the world through a different set of eyes. People really can evolve into their greatness—I see it every day.

The people or circumstances that take you out of your power have extraordinary value: They reveal your limiting beliefs, fears and false assumptions.

Kahlil Gibran, one of my favorite thinkers, once wrote: "I have learned silence from the talkative, toleration from the intolerant, and kindness from the unkind; yet, strange, I am grateful to those teachers." So the next time a co-worker sets you off or your teenager gets you going, or the next time a rude waiter in a restaurant makes you angry, walk over to them, give them a hug. Thank them for the gift they just gave you. Because, in truth, they really did.

50

Speak like a Superstar

The words you use determine the way you feel. The language you choose shapes the way you perceive reality. Your vocabulary drives meaning in your life. Please think about this idea. I believe it's a big one.

The superstar businesspeople who I've coached are among the most high-spirited people I've ever met. And the way they talk reflects that devotion to being an uplifter and elevator of human beings. They wouldn't dream of calling a setback a "problem"—they'd call it an "opportunity to create something even greater." And then, as if by magic, their positive language provokes a set of positive sensations within them that supports them in playing victor versus victim in the seemingly difficult situation. The great ones among us would never express information about an upset customer as "bad news" but instead would label it "a challenge that will help us grow." Rather than using negative words, they prefer winning words that inspire those around them to dwell in possibility and keep their heads focused on the dream. The words you use influence the life you live. Select them wisely.

I have a little exercise to offer you. Pull out your journal or a clean white sheet of paper and record an inventory of the words you most frequently speak. The more aware you can become of the quality of your language, the more choice you will give yourself. And writing things down dramatically raises your self-awareness. Then, once you have identified your most commonly used words, do another list. Articulate a series of spectacularly positive words that will serve you—words that you imagine a superstar in your field using. Bring them into your daily vocabulary. You will discover that speaking these words will make you feel better. More powerful. More passionate. And when you feel great feelings, guess what? You'll do great things.

The words you use influence the life you live. Select them wisely.

51

Learning or Decaying

There's a cure for aging that no one talks about. It's called learning. In my mind, as long as you learn something new each day, stretch your personal frontiers and improve the way you think, you cannot grow old. Aging only happens to people who lose their lust for getting better and disconnect from their natural base of curiosity. "Every three or four years I pick a new subject. It may be Japanese art; it may be economics. Three years of study are by no means enough to master a subject but they are enough to understand it. So for more than 60 years I have kept studying one subject at a time," said Peter Drucker, the father of modern management who lived until he was 95. Brilliant guy.

Last year, I had the joy of spending a couple of hours in conversation with Shimon Peres, the former Israeli prime minister and Nobel Peace Prize winner. He was nearly 82 at the time, and I couldn't help but notice that his eyes actually sparkled as he spoke of his love of books, big ideas and learning. I asked: "Mr. Peres, when do you read?" His reply: "Robin, when don't I read? I read when I get up in the morning, when I can during the day and every single evening. Most of my weekends are spent reading great books. Books are my constant companions." He then added with a smile: "If you eat three times a day you'll be fed. But if you read three times a day you'll be wise."

Too many people never pick up a book after they've finished school. Unbelievable. Too many people spend more time watching TV than getting deep inside the minds of the greatest people who have walked the planet. Too many people have closed their minds to new insights and powerful thoughts. One idea discovered in one book can change the way you see the world. One idea read in one book could transform the way you communicate with people. One idea found in one book could help you live longer or be happier or drive your business to remarkable success. Never leave home without a book in your hand.

There's a cure for aging that no one talks about. It's called learning.

52

Simple Tactics for Superb Relationships

Any good psychologist will tell you that one of the deepest needs of a human being is the need to belong. We are happiest when we feel connected to others—when we are part of a community. Top performers in business make it a priority to build relationships with their teammates and their customers. Connecting with the people who surround them is not seen as a waste of time; instead, it is an exquisitely wise use of their time.

As a leadership development specialist, I work with our corporate clients to build cultures where people and relationships come first. This promotes communication, collaboration and strong business results. When people feel appreciated, they shine. Here are 10 deceptively simple ideas for building your human connections that have helped employees of the companies that engage us for leadership coaching get to a whole new level of high performance:

1. *Be the most positive person you know.*
2. *Be candid and speak truthfully.*

3. *Be on time.*

4. *Say please and thank you.*

5. *Under-promise and over-deliver.*

6. *Leave people better than you found them.*

7. *Be friendly and caring.*

8. *Be a world-class listener.*

9. *Become passionately interested in other people.*

10. *Smile a lot.*

One of the deepest needs of a **human** being is the need to **belong**.

Here's a bonus point: Treat people with respect—always. I've discovered a very powerful law that just may change the way you lead as well as the way you live: To get respect, give respect. I sometimes share a story of a respected consultant who was engaged—at a great sum of money—to reveal his many years of wisdom with the management team of a large organization. The consultant walked into the meeting room and looked intensely at the group. He then reached for a marker and wrote four words on the whiteboard behind him: "Treat people with respect." He smiled at the executives. And then he left.

53

Rock Stars as Poets

I love music. I find music just makes life better. Add a little music to an ordinary experience and it becomes extraordinary. I just drove my kids to school before I wrote this chapter. Played the new Our Lady Peace CD as we drove. My daughter, Bianca, looked up at me and said: "Daddy, music makes me feel like dancing." Her eyes sparkled as she said it. Perfect.

Last night I had a thoughtful conversation with an interesting friend. He makes his living in the financial markets. But he lives his passion spinning turntables as a DJ. Cool combination. He loves music. Makes his life better too. We talked about Morcheeba and Thievery Corporation and U2 and the Dave Matthews Band. That got me thinking. Music can connect us, giving us a shared language, whether we live in New York or Bogotá, Tel Aviv, San Juan, Bangalore or Beijing. Music has the potential to elevate our lives, enrich our societies and uplift the world.

Here's what I really think: Musicians are artists, no different from painters or poets. They document our culture, cause us to think, provoke us (sometimes) and introduce us to new ideas. And the good ones are philosophers. Seriously. The best share wise insights through their songs that inspire us to see the

world through a new set of lenses and step out of the ordinary—
into the realm of something special—if only for three minutes.

Bono of U2 said in an interview that he sees himself as
a traveling salesman. He crisscrosses the planet selling a message, evangelizing his values, spreading the silent whispers of his
heart on a stage in front of tens of thousands. Bono's a poet. Just
read some of his stuff. It's deep. Alanis Morissette also comes to
mind when I think of lyrics with philosophical weight. So does
Dave Matthews. Even Eminem's words, when not profane, have
power. Listen to them sometime. The guy gets life.

Musicians are artists, no different from painters or poets. They document our culture, cause us to think, provoke us (sometimes) and introduce us to new ideas. And the good ones are philosophers.

So let me ask you: Do you fill your moments with music?
What songs make you think or laugh or cry? What music makes
your heart soar and reminds you how beautifully blessed you are
to be walking the planet today? What tunes inspire you to reach
higher, dream bigger and get to the greatness that you are meant
to be? Oh, and let me ask you one final question: What is the
music that makes you just want to get up and start dancing?

54

The Innovator's Mantra

True innovators have a mantra: "The enemy of the best is the good." They are constantly daring to make things better. What others call impossible they see as probable. They live out of their imaginations—not their memories. They live to challenge the commonly accepted. They assume nothing. They see no limits. To them, everything's possible.

If you want to be a leader, I have a simple suggestion: Just keep innovating. Innovate at work. Innovate at home. Innovate in your relationships. Innovate in the way you run your life. Innovate in terms of the way you see the world. To become stagnant is to begin to die. Growth, evolution and reinvention sustain life. Sure it can be scary. But wouldn't you rather feel your fear than play small with your life?

There's no safety in being the same person today that you were yesterday. That's just an illusion that ends up breaking your heart when you get to the end of your life and realize that you missed out on living it boldly. Lasting fulfillment lives out in the unknown. When I was a kid, my dad used to tell me: "Robin, it's risky out on the limb. But, son—that's where all the fruit is." And to play out on the skinny branch, you need to innovate. Daily. Relentlessly.

Of course, the more you innovate and refuse to be bound by the chains of complacency, the more you will fail. I mentioned that in an earlier chapter. Not every risk you take and not everything you try will work out as planned. That's just life happening. Failure truly is essential to success. And the more you stretch, the farther you will reach. Failure is a gift anyway. Failure has been so helpful to me. It's taken me closer to my dreams, equipped me with more knowledge and toughened me up so I'm more prepared. Success and failure go hand in hand. They are business partners.

There's no safety in being the same person today that you were yesterday. That's just an illusion that ends up breaking your heart.

One of pharmaceutical giant GlaxoSmithKline's organizing values is "disturb." Love it. Makes me think of the words of Motorola CEO Ed Zander: "At the height of success, 'break' your business. Companies that don't innovate don't survive, so the key is driving this innovation. The lesson is especially important when things are going well. Though it's counterintuitive, successful companies actually need to be more innovative than the competition. It's like kids playing king of the hill—everyone aims for the kid at the top. Leaders that don't innovate are displaced by those willing to take risks." So go to work each day and refuse to do the same thing you did yesterday—just because it was what you did yesterday. Keep challenging yourself to think better, do better and be better. Shake thinks up. Confront your limitations. Refuse to be average. Stand for what's best. Commit to being breathtakingly great in all you do. And that's what you'll become. Sooner than you think.

55

Pleasure vs. Happiness

Pleasure is great—but it doesn't last. Pleasure comes from your five senses. From a great meal, a nice glass of wine and a new car. Nothing wrong with these things—they make the experience of life better. But they are fleeting.

Pleasure comes from something on the outside. Happiness comes from within.

Happiness, well, that's a different story. Happiness is the DNA of pleasure. My point is simply this: Pleasure comes from something on the outside. Happiness comes from within. It's a state you create by choice. It's a decision. It's an act of will.

People can be happy when they are going through great pain and adversity. There's no pleasure evident in their external lives and yet they are content on the inside. And, conversely, tons of people are surrounded by pleasure (fast cars, nice homes, great clothes) but there's no joy within. So choose to be happy. You can't control life on the outside. Hard stuff will happen. But you can control what goes on inside. And those who do become great.

56

The $600 Sandwich

Never a dull moment in my life. I just got back from lunch. I went out to pick up a sub sandwich from my usual place. Get this: When I checked my receipt after swiping my debit card, the bill said $577.89. They sell great sandwiches, but that was a bit rich for my blood.

A couple of leadership lessons I want to offer you from this little escapade:

OAD. *Great businesses are remarkably detail oriented. I love what Stephen Jay Gould once said: "Details are all that matters; God dwells in these and you never get to see Him if you don't struggle to get them right." At our company, we talk about OAD: Obsessive Attention to Detail. The best organizations I've worked with sweat the small stuff. They understand that customers notice every little detail. The woman behind the counter was not being present in the moment. She should have punched in $5.77. Big boo-boo. And her boss was standing next to her. Oops. I was gracious and helped her save face. Many wouldn't have.*

TAKE PERSONAL RESPONSIBILITY *(and do it fast). When I checked the bill and saw the (outrageous) error, I mentioned it to the* *woman politely. Her reply was classic: "Didn't you check before you okayed the amount?" No one wants to take responsibility for things anymore. We blame everyone else. After a few minutes, she got her wisdom back and apologized profusely. I know she just got scared when she saw what she'd done. And most of us, when we get scared, blame others to avoid the pain of owning the mistake we've made.*

PAY ATTENTION. *Glad I checked my bill. Sometimes I don't because my mind is up in the clouds, dreaming about how to change the world. But world-class leaders are attentive. They reside in the moment.*

The best organizations I've worked with sweat the small stuff.

I'll go back to this place. The owner gave me the sub for free and they all felt bad. But their credibility has been seriously undermined and they'll need to earn my trust back. I pray they will because they make really good sandwiches.

57

Good Business Is Good for Business

Here's a simple idea that will have a fantastic impact on your organization (and your career) once you act on it: People want to work for a good company—one that is not only well-run but that does its part to build a better world. Being a good business is good for business. That's not some cheesy slogan I just came up with—that's what I've observed, having worked with real people at real companies around the world. The best companies have a noble purpose and a clear intent to treat their people and their customers well. Great companies also understand that while it's mission-critical to be hugely profitable, it's also mission-critical to be socially responsible. Many of our clients have set up programs to help the disadvantaged or to make communities better. I admire them more than they will ever know.

Pride is something that doesn't get talked about much in business circles. Too bad. What I've discovered is that people want to go to work each day with pride in their hearts. They want to feel good about the company they work for. They want to know that their company—and the work they do—

elevates lives and makes a difference. Business philosopher Peter Koestenbaum expressed it so well in his excellent book *Leadership: The Inner Side of Greatness*: "Business is above all a vehicle for achieving personal and organization greatness. It is for accomplishing something worthy and noble. Business is an institution that can enable you to make significant contributions to society."

People want to work for a good company—one that is not only well-run but that does its part to build a better world.

As I've suggested throughout this book, we all can lead without title. We all have an impact. We all can do good, at work—and in our communities. So become a volunteer. Give money to charities. Start to tithe (the word actually means one-tenth, or 10%) your income to good causes. And as an organization, engage in projects that help communities in need (by setting up a foundation or by supporting important initiatives). Become dedicated to making a greater contribution. Stand for social responsibility as well as remarkable profitability. Not only will you retain your top talent and attract even more, but your customers will respect you. Good business really is good for business. And giving really does begin the receiving process.

58

Build Success Structures

Yesterday, on my way in to work, I pulled up next to one of those big new Mercedes sedans. The man driving it had his windows rolled down a bit so I heard the song blaring through his stereo system: Queen's "We Are the Champions." Made me think of a CEO who attended one of the leadership summits we run a couple of times a year. He operates a major company. Wanted to improve his organization along with his life. Told me he listens to AC/DC's "Back in Black" full blast before his big sales calls. Interesting.

What practices get you to your best? What rituals throw you into your best game mode? What tactics inspire you to really get going to let your bright light shine? We all need what I call Success Structures scheduled into our weeks to ensure we stay at our highest. We all need systems installed into our days to ensure consistency of results, order and superb outcomes. The best companies have systems to ensure quality control—so should you. Get serious about building systems and you'll show you're serious about success. Things that work for me, as I've suggested, include lots of exercise, high-energy music, reading great books, weekly meetings—even if for only 15 minutes on the phone—with inspirational friends and writing in my journal. They get built into my week just like my most important meetings (and time with my kids).

We all need **systems** installed into our days to ensure consistency of results, order and **superb** outcomes.

Success doesn't just occur. It's a project that is worked on each day. You need to swim out to it. You need to make it happen (along with letting it happen—once you've given your best). As Václav Havel once observed: "Vision is not enough; it must be combined with venture. It is not enough to stare up to the step; we must step up the stairs." So what will you do today to jump-start yourself? Don't postpone your greatness. Your time is now. And if not now, then when?

59

The Person Who Experiences Most Wins

Big idea: Why wait to get old to become experienced? I want the experience of an old man while I'm still young. And I think I've figured out a way to get it: Collapse the timeline. Most people don't take that many risks or have that many new conversations or read that many new books or take that many new travels. By engaging in these and other experience-building pursuits at a dramatically accelerated rate, I figure I could get 10 years' worth of learning and lessons in a quarter of the time. Just collapse the timeline by doing more important stuff faster and sooner. Just stay focused and committed. Just put more living into each of my days.

We all get the same allotment of time. Each of us gets 24 hours each day. The sad fact is that too many among us spend too much time doing unimportant things. Living reactive lives. Saying "yes" to activities they should be saying "no" to. Drifting like a piece of wood in a river, moving in whatever direction the current happens to be moving on that particular day. All because they did not make the time to think. About their priorities. About their dreams and goals. And to note what they want to make of their lives. People have lost 20 good years this way. Seriously.

By getting clear on what you want out of life, you heighten your awareness around what's most important. With better awareness comes better choices. And with better choices you'll see better results. Clarity breeds success.

So don't wait until the end of your life to become experienced. Collapse the timeline. Get clear on what you need to experience to have a fulfilling life—and then start doing it now. Meet cool people. Visit neat places. Read deep books. Seize opportunities. Fail often—it reflects an increase in your reach and risk-taking. Who cares if you win or lose, so long as you get another experience to add to the inventory. Even the saddest of times make your life richer. Benjamin Zander, the conductor of the Boston Philharmonic, shared the following line from his teacher, the great cellist Gaspar Cassadó, in his wonderful book *The Art of Possibility*: "I'm so sorry for you; your lives have been so easy. You can't play great music unless your heart's been broken."

I want the experience of an old man while I'm still young. And I think I've figured out a way to get it: Collapse the timeline.

The more experiences, the better the life. The person who experiences most wins.

60

Brand like Diddy

This morning just after I woke up, I chilled out. Listened to some Coltrane, a dose of Sade and then played some music by Diddy (the artist formerly known as Puff Daddy then P. Diddy; my name seems so boring now). I needed something to jump-start my day (and wake up the kids). Reflecting on him and the business empire he's built got me thinking. About brands.

To win in your marketspace, your organization needs to develop a magnificently cherished and superbly respected brand. (I mentioned Kevin Roberts, CEO of Saatchi & Saatchi, in an earlier chapter; he doesn't even use the term "brand" anymore, preferring "lovemark." Nice.) And for you to get to professional greatness, I suggest that you work on, polish and protect your personal brand: your good name. (It could take you 30 years to build a great reputation—and 30 seconds to lose it, with one act of poor judgment.)

Everyone's into brand-building these days. Law firms. Accounting enterprises. Retail organizations. Paris Hilton recently said: "I'm a brand."

This raises the question: "How can we get our brand from where it now is to where we want it to be?" My answer is simple: Model Diddy.

Sure you can read the books out there (lots of excellent ones, such as Seth Godin's *Purple Cow* and *The 22 Immutable Laws of Branding* by Al Ries and his daughter Laura Ries). And sure you can invest in getting your brand managers to world class (every company should have brand managers). But I'll save you some money with a simple suggestion: Study hip hop artists like Diddy and 50 Cent and Jay-Z (whom *Fortune* recently called "America's Hippest CEO"). You'll learn all you need to learn about taking a brand to the top of the mountain. These guys are amazing. Constantly reinventing. Relentlessly innovating. Endlessly improving. They have one hit record that drives their name—their brand, sorry—into the public consciousness and then extend their line into clothes, books, movies, colognes, etc. Study the way they build community, cement loyalty and tattoo what they stand for onto people's brain cells.

I'll leave you with an unforgettable quote from Jay-Z: "I'm not a businessman. I'm a business, man."

61

Get Big into Blessings

"I cursed the fact I had no shoes until I met a man who had no feet." Comes from a Persian proverb. That line sends shivers down my spine. Whoever wrote that really gets it. It's easy to fall into the very human trap of focusing on what we don't have rather than being grateful for what we do have. I'll bet you have more blessings in your life than you are noticing.

A billion children went to sleep hungry last night. People in the world lost family members yesterday whom they adored. There are people in your own community dying of cancer and AIDS. I just read about a little girl who was born without a face. Just two eyes and a mouth. And we worry about traffic being heavy on the way to work.

I just read about a **little girl** who was born without a face. Just two eyes and a mouth. And we worry about **traffic** being heavy on the way into work.

Here's a word to think about: perspective. Travel to more countries and you'll get greater perspective on our world. Talk to people you've never talked to and you'll get a new perspective on what life can be. And celebrate the blessings in your life and you'll reconnect with how fortunate you are. It's human nature not to appreciate all we have until it's lost. Fight that urge.

62

Be Wise, Early Rise

I gave the keynote address at a conference for the leadership team of the telephone banking division of CIBC yesterday. Great group. CIBC is one of Canada's leading banks and the audience was full of energy, passion and intelligence. I shared my ideas on building a high-performance culture, developing deeper relationships and the power of leading without title. Then I offered some insights on personal leadership—beginning with the imperative of getting up early if one wants to get to world class as a human being. The room fell silent. Thought I'd lost them.

I love connecting personally with audience members and happily stayed after my presentation to answer questions. Amazing how many people asked me what they needed to do to build the early rising habit. "I want to get a lot more from life," one manager said. "I loved your point about taking a 'holy hour' each morning—60 minutes to feed my mind, care for my body and develop my character," said another. "Life is passing by so quickly," noted yet another, "I really need to start getting up earlier to get more from my days."

It's so easy to forget that our outer lives reflect our inner lives and that by getting up earlier each day to do some internal work, our days will become dramatically better. How can you be a positive source of energy to those around you when you have no energy? How can you develop the best in others if you haven't connected with the best within yourself? And how can you champion another person if you fail to see the champion in you? Getting up early to do your inner work, enlarge your thinking, to sharpen your life's philosophy or to review your goals is not a waste of time. That 'holy hour' infuses every remaining minute of your day with a perspective that elevates each area of your life. It'll transform you. Make you better as a leader. As a parent. As a human being. Here are six practical tactics to help you get up early (5 a.m. is nice):

DON'T EAT AFTER 7 P.M. *You will sleep more deeply as well as more sweetly. It's the quality, not the quantity, of sleep that's most important.*

DON'T LOUNGE IN BED *after your alarm clock goes off. Jump out of bed and start your day. The more time you lie in bed after the alarm clock goes off, the greater the likelihood that the chatter of your mind will say something like, "Stay in bed. Sleep a bit more. The bed is warm. You deserve it."*

GET INTO WORLD-CLASS PHYSICAL CONDITION. *This is a big idea. I find that when I am in excellent physical shape—working out five to six times a week and eating ultra-well—it is easy to jump out of bed at 5 a.m. or even 4 a.m. Being superbly fit is a brilliant move that will positively influence every area of your life.*

SET BHAGs. *Jim Collins coined the term "BHAGs," meaning Big Hairy Audacious Goals, in his book* Built to Last. *Goals breathe life and energy into your days. Most people don't get up early because they* have no reason to. *The secret of passion (and getting up early) is purpose.* Goals inspire you and give you something to get out of bed for each morning. Taking out your journal and articulating 10-, 5-, 3- and 1-year goals for the core dimensions of your life will focus your mind and drive tremendous results. It will light a fire in your belly and flood you with passion.

SET YOUR ALARM CLOCK 30 MINUTES FAST. *I shared this point at a recent "Awakening Best Self Weekend," a workshop where people come from all around the world to learn how to break through their fears and live their greatest lives. I just got an email from one participant from Spain. This little trick has completely changed her life. She thinks she's getting up at 6 a.m. By the time she's up and out of bed, she realizes it's only 5:30 a.m. She uses the newfound time to meditate or read or to exercise. She cares for her inner life now and the results have been excellent. Her business is more successful than it's ever been. Her family life is at its best place in years. And she's feeling incredibly happy. I know this tactic seems silly—but it works.*

So join the 5 O'clock Club. Win the Battle of the Bed. Put mind over mattress. Get up early.

GIVE IT 30 DAYS. *One of my favorite clients is NASA. They are doing our* Grow The Leader *program to develop the leadership capabilities of their people. I love this organization because it truly stands for world class. One of the things I've learned from NASA is that the space shuttle uses more fuel during the first few minutes after liftoff than it* *consumes during its entire trip around the globe. Why? Because, initially, it needs to overcome the tremendous pull of gravity. But as it does—it gets easier to fly. That's a powerful thought to consider. Personal change is a process that can be hardest at the beginning. It doesn't happen in a day or even a week. It takes time to overcome the pull of your old habits. But after four weeks from today your life could be so much better, if you choose. Always give yourself 30 days to install a new habit.*

So join the 5 O'clock Club. Win the Battle of the Bed. Put mind over mattress. Get up early. And remember what Benjamin Franklin once noted: "There will be plenty of time to sleep when you are dead." Smart guy.

63

Who Made Success a Dirty Word?

Too many people believe that there's something wrong with aiming to be really successful. Too many people put down productive achievement. Too many people snicker at go-getters who set their goals and then devote themselves to realizing them. I've heard it a lot these days, the suggestion that if you strive for success, you must not be all that concerned with making a difference and being significant. It's almost as if being a go-getter is incompatible with being compassionate, socially conscious and a good person. Nonsense.

Here's my take on the "success versus significance" issue: An extraordinary life contains both. The essence of life is balance. Without success, I have a sense that the best part of you will feel a little hollow. Part of what makes us human is the hunger to realize our greatest gifts and to live life fully. We were built to be great. And high achievement is simply a reflection of creativity in action. The more worthwhile things you are doing, the more of your natural creativity you are unleashing. Success is a creative act. It's also one of the best routes to fulfillment, if blended with a healthy respect for work-life balance. I've found that few things feel as great as the feeling I get when I complete something worthwhile. Doing important things promotes happiness. Success awakens joy. And yet without significance, I believe that we will feel that we have walked the planet in vain. Success alone, without feeling that you've made a meaningful contribution, will leave the heart feeling empty.

While you chase success, I urge you to stay devoted to elevating the lives you touch and leaving your world better than you found it.

There's nothing wrong with being an elite performer and taking the steps required to become a remarkable success in this world. Success is actually a reflection of healthy self-esteem. But while you chase success, I urge you to stay devoted to elevating the lives you touch and leaving your world better than you found it. That's the significance piece. With both, you'll discover your greatest life.

64

Get Great at Life

Life is a skill. And like any other skill, once you know the ground rules and make the time to practice, you can get better. A lot better. If you really devote yourself to life, you could even reach a place of mastery. Some have.

I suggest that there are three simple things you can do to get great at life:

PAY ATTENTION TO LIFE. *Make the time to reflect on what you want your life to stand for, what you have learned from your years and what your legacy will be. Time slips through our fingers—like grains of sand—never to return again. Use your days to realize your talents. Makes me think of that line by Erma Bombeck: "When I stand before God at the end of my life, I would hope that I would not have a single bit of talent left and could say, 'I used everything you gave me.'" Try to write in a journal each morning before you walk out into your world. Think about what goals you need to accomplish for you to feel the day has been a success—and write them down. Think about your most closely held values. Think about what lessons you've learned from the previous day. What good is making a mistake if you don't learn from it?*

ENGAGE IN LIFE. *Angelina Jolie spoke truth when she said: "The* *only way to have a life is to commit to it like crazy." I've learned some-thing as I've grown older: Life returns what you give it. Donate your best. Over dinner last night with some friends, we began to speak of goal-setting. "But why set goals when life can be so uncertain?" one friend asked. My reply: "Just because life is so unpredictable doesn't mean you shouldn't exercise your power to be great. Set your goals. Make your plans. Take action and chase your dreams. That's what personal responsibility is all about. But once you've done your best—let go. And let life do the rest."*

At the **end**, the billionaire gets buried next to the street sweeper. We **all** end up as dust. So let's have some fun.

ENJOY LIFE. *We take life so seriously. But at the end, the billionaire gets buried next to the street sweeper. We all end up as dust. So let's have some fun. "Few of us write great novels," observed Mignon McLaughlin. "But all of us can live them."*

65

The Steve Jobs Question

Steve Jobs is an interesting guy. How many people start a billion-dollar business in their garage in their early twenties? How many people can lead the field in three separate industries? (Music—the iPod has revolutionized the way music is delivered; movies—Pixar is one of the world's most successful animation studios; and computing—Apple's devotion to sexy design and ease of use is legendary.) But what intrigues me most about Steve Jobs is his philosophy.

Jobs asks himself an unforgettable question every time he is faced with a big choice: "What would I do if this was the last night of my life?" Powerful idea behind that. He met his wife that way.

He was giving a university address a number of years back. She was sitting in the audience. He fell for her and approached her after the event. She gave him her number. He wanted to take her out to dinner that very night but had a business meeting on the books. Life's like that. On his way back to his car, he asked himself what I call the Steve Jobs Question: "What would I do if this was the last night of my life?" You and I both know his answer. He ran back to the auditorium, found the woman and took her out. They've been together ever since.

What would I do if this was the last night of my life?

Look, I know we all have to be practical. I get that we can't apply Jobs' question to every situation. But as I wrote in *Who Will Cry When You Die?*, connecting to your mortality is a great source of wisdom. Reminding yourself that in the overall scheme of things you will not be here that long—no matter how long you live—is an excellent way to drive passion, promote risk-taking and get deeply into the game of life. Connecting with the end is a brilliant practice to keep you focused on what's most important. Before it's too late.

66

What's Missing from Your Coolness?

I was just out skateboarding with my daughter. Today I bought her a new helmet, arm pads and boarding sneakers. She looks like a pro. Now she just needs to learn how to ride the thing.

She loves her new accessories. To her, skateboarding is ultra-hip and the perfect sport. So we were out there, having fun, when she looked up at me and said: "Dad, there's something missing from my coolness." What a line. Hilarious. Got me thinking.

What's missing from my coolness? What's missing from my authenticity? What's missing from my greatest life? Awareness precedes choice and choice precedes results. (Okay, I'll stop repeating that line; it's just that it's so incredibly important.) With better awareness of what needs to improve in your life, you can make better choices. And with better choices, you will see better results. We truly cannot eliminate weaknesses we don't even know about.

One of our biggest regrets on our deathbeds is that we were not reflective enough. That we didn't spend enough time thinking, in deep contemplation. Don't let that happen to you. Make the time to think. Ask yourself what needs to improve in your life. Ask yourself what needs to get done. Ask yourself what values you need to live. Ask yourself how exceptional are you, how "plugged in" are you, how interesting (and interested) are you—how cool are you? Then make your life your message. And don't let anything be missing from your coolness.

One of our biggest regrets on our deathbeds is that we were not reflective enough.

67

No Ask, No Get

I'm on an airplane as I write this chapter. I love being at 35,000 feet. No distractions. No interruptions. Pure think time. Only one problem—I forgot my water. I'll explain.

One of my best practices around flying is drinking a ton of water while in the sky. I'll drink a liter easily. It prevents dehydration, keeps me energized and maintains sharpness of mind. I get many of my biggest ideas on airplanes. And when I get off the plane, rather than being tired, I go straight home to do fun stuff with my kids. But before this flight—because I was rushing to make my connection—I missed my ritual. I didn't buy my *agua*. So guess what I did? I asked for some.

It never hurts to ask.

I walked over to the flight attendant and explained that I drink a lot of water and wondered whether he could help out, if there was an extra big bottle of the good stuff on board. I know they usually only provide a glass or two, but I fiercely believe that it never hurts to ask. To me, that's an organizing principle I try to live my life by—and it's served me so well. I was polite. I wasn't pushy. I just asked for what I wanted.

"With pleasure," came the reply. And with that he walked over to a metal trolley, opened it up and pulled out the prize: a 1.5 liter bottle of Vittel water. Perfect. So here I sit, nice and hydrated. Listening to Boozoo Bajou's awesome CD *Dust My Broom* on my iPod and reading *The Spirit to Serve*, J.W. Marriott's book on how the hotel chain got where it is. No jet lag for me from this flight. No chance. Because I asked.

68

Sell Your Desk

The best performers in business don't hide behind their desks. They know that business is all about connecting to people. When people like you and know you and trust you, they will help you. Just the way it is. Human nature at play.

The best managers get out from behind their desks and have rich and meaningful conversations with their team. They get that passion is contagious and, before someone will lend you their hand, you need to touch their heart. The best salespeople get out from behind their desks and break bread with their customers. They understand the power of relationship-selling. (Big idea: People don't buy products and services—they buy people and relationships.) The best employees get out from behind their desks to collaborate with their teammates, support their colleagues and to spread their enthusiasm.

The best **performers** in business don't hide behind their desks. They know that business is all about connecting to **people**.

More than ever in my own life, I try to get out of the office. I love my team but they know what they are doing. They don't need me there anymore. They lead without title and are empowered. I'll just get in their way if I'm around too much. I need to be out meeting my much-cherished readers. I need to be out serving my beloved clients and helping them build world-class organizations. I need to be out learning new ideas and interesting insights that will find their way onto my blog or my podcasts or into my next speech or book. Hiding behind my desk is the worst place I could be. The "paperless office"? It'll never happen in my lifetime. The "deskless office"? Give me a year.

69

Get Fit to Lead

You know I'm an evangelist around the whole idea of being ultra-fit if you want to be at your best. Getting into world-class physical condition is one of the smartest moves you can make. Exercising will make you look better, feel stronger and fill you with boundless energy. Staying fit will even make you happier.

The past week has been a time of great change for me. I'm reengineering my business to make it more focused and fast. I'm coaching my team so that they know the new standards and goals. I'm pushing myself harder to get more done and generate better results. And I'm lifting the bar on the size of my dreams. I need to make a bigger difference. I passionately feel that. As I go through all this, one of the practices that is serving me so well is my daily pilgrimage to the gym.

I remember a professional speaker named Peter Urs Bender once telling me: "Robin, some people go to church each day. Well, my church is the gym. And each day that's where I go to get blessed." I also remember a participant in one of my leadership seminars sharing: "Exercise is an insurance policy I've taken out on my health. And each day that I go into the gym, I'm paying the premium." Yet another person told me recently at a book signing: "Good health is a crown on the head of a well person that only a sick person can see." Smart points. Wise people.

No matter how busy I get or how much pressure is on my shoulders, a good workout makes me feel at ease. I come off the treadmill feeling relaxed, full of joy and with a sense of perspective over the issues on my plate. I get so many big ideas while I'm running and such clarity while I'm lifting weights. And staying fit keeps me happy and positive. Look, I know I'll never be Mr. Universe. But because I care for my health, my life will be a lot better, more productive and longer than if I didn't. And that's good enough for me.

"Good health is a **crown** on the head of a well person that only a sick person can **see**."

70

Extreme Leadership and Kids' Clothing

I just had a visit with the tailor who adjusts my kids' school clothes this morning before I wrote this chapter. I've known him for a long time and he's always treated us well. He's been in business for 40 years, so I thought I'd get behind his eyeballs and discover what has made his business both as successful and as sustainable as it's been. I started asking my questions.

Always be getting and doing better. Never settle for mediocrity.

"Robin, there are four simple principles that we've followed here in our shop. They've served me well my whole life. I actually learned them by watching my mother as I grew up. She was one of the most amazing people I've ever known," he said, and then paused for a moment. "I miss her terribly."

I thought I'd share Neil's four principles with you, as you raise your standards and shine more brightly at work—and at home.

FOUR LEADERSHIP LESSONS FROM A WISE TAILOR:

IMPROVE. *Always be getting and doing better. Never settle for mediocrity.*

OBSERVE. *Talk to the people you work with. Really listen to them. And keep your eyes on the business. Because you can expect only that which you inspect.*

CONNECT. *Be really good to people. Treat your customers with respect. Give them good value. Be caring and deal with any complaints fast.*

ADAPT. *Conditions change. Competition grows. Uncertainty is the new normal. Stay fast. Stay flexible. Stay nimble.*

71

The Seven Forms of Wealth

I just gave a full-day leadership seminar attended by managers and executives of companies like American Express, Infosys, The Gap and Dell. One of the ideas that many of the people in the room told me was most helpful was my "Seven Forms of Wealth" model that I've been sharing with our corporate clients over the past year.

In my mind, wealth isn't just about making money. There are actually seven elements that you want to raise to world-class levels before you call yourself rich. I'll identify them:

INNER WEALTH. *This includes a positive mindset, high self-respect, internal peace and a strong spiritual connection.*

PHYSICAL WEALTH. *Your health is your wealth. What's the point of getting to a great place in your career if you get sick doing it? Why be the best businessperson in the hospital ward? Why be the richest person in the graveyard?*

FAMILY AND SOCIAL WEALTH. *When your family life is happy, you will perform better at work. No one gets to the end of their life and regrets making their family their first priority. Related to this is* the imperative of forging deep connections with friends and members of your personal community (including mentors, role models and trusted advisors).

CAREER WEALTH. Actualizing your highest potential by reaching for your best in your career is incredibly important. Getting to greatness in your profession brings a feeling of satisfaction on a job well done. It helps you make your mark. Being world class in your work is so good for your self-respect.

ECONOMIC WEALTH. Yes, money is important. Not the most important thing in life but very important. It absolutely makes life easier and better. Money allows you to live in a nice home, take beautiful vacations and provide well for those you love. And as Yvon Chouinard, the founder of the outdoor gear company Patagonia, has said: "The more I make, the more I can give away."

There are actually seven elements that you want to raise to world-class levels before you call yourself rich.

ADVENTURE WEALTH. To be fulfilled, each of us needs mystery in our lives. Challenge is necessary for happiness. The human brain craves novelty. And we are creative beings so we need to be creating constantly if we hope to feel joy. Lots of adventure (ranging from meeting new people to visiting new places) is an essential element of authentic wealth.

IMPACT WEALTH. *Perhaps the deepest longing of the human heart is to live for something greater than itself. Each of us craves to be significant. To make a difference. To know that the world has somehow been better because we have walked the planet. Think of what Richard Bach once wrote: "Here is the test to find whether your mission on earth is finished: If you're alive, it isn't."*

I invite you to focus on each of these seven elements if you want to experience *real* wealth. Money alone does not define being wealthy. There are many rich people who are unhappy and unsuccessful as human beings. By focusing on elevating all seven of these areas to world-class levels, you will not only shine ever so brightly for all those around you—you will also find a contentment that lasts.

72

Apply the U2 Standard

U2 is one of the coolest rock bands in the world. But that's not the main reason I love them. Yes, their music is fantastic. Yes, their songs are often profound. Yes, their live performances are brilliant (just watch their DVD *Go Home: Live from Slane Castle* if you have any doubt). But what really draws me to U2 is their unrelenting commitment to getting better—no matter how great they become. It's not about the money for them. It's not about the fame. It's not about getting on magazine covers. It's mostly about refusing to accept anything less than mastery as their standard. As Bono observed: "That's the thing about U2. The band always feels like it's coming, never that it's arrived." Beautiful.

All great leaders, serial innovators, successful entrepreneurs and superstar creatives have that ever-present longing deep within their souls to do, be and see something special during their lives. Every single one of them has that fire in her belly. Sure you could call their insatiable hunger somewhat unhealthy and suggest that such people lack contentment. And you'd be right. But as I suggested in an earlier chapter, these are the very people who have given us the progress of the world, these are the men and women who have built spectacular businesses and organizations that add value to our lives. The people who have provided us with the genius inventions that make things easier. The scientists who help us live with better health and longer lifespans. The human beings who have allowed us the chance to witness beautiful art and wonderful music. Greatness arrives for those who are never satisfied with what is, no matter how nice it looks. Yes, one must find happiness in life. And we need to enjoy the journey. Definitely. I evangelize that message everywhere I go. Life balance is unbelievably important.

All I'm saying is that too many among us have gone to the other extreme. Chasing happiness, inner peace and balance while leaving the natural instinct to create something spectacular at the side of life's highway like yesterday's roadkill. In doing so, they've fallen out of balance. And missed out on one of the main reasons to be alive: to create. To shine. To be great.

Greatness arrives for those who are never satisfied with what is, no matter how nice it looks.

So apply the U2 Standard. Each day—and every day until you take your last breath. Feel like you are coming—never that you've arrived. Strive for mastery and brilliance and excellence, in all that you do. You'll join the realm of those rare individuals who reached the end feeling few regrets and little remorse. You'll delight in the fact that you squeezed out the best from life and played out loud. You'll feel that true sense of happiness that all of us aspire to but so few of us ever reach. And guess what else? When you're in heaven's waiting room—you just might get to meet Bono.

73

Learn More to Earn More

A simple idea to move to your next level: To earn more you must learn more. The compensation you receive from your employer will be determined by the value you add. The more you know, the more valuable you become. To earn more, learn more. Out-read your competition. Out-study them. Out-improve them. Out-succeed them.

I remember when I was a lawyer, just starting my professional career. I asked the top lawyer at the firm what I needed to do to ensure a sustained career there. I've never forgotten his reply: "Robin, be so knowledgeable, competent and brilliant at what you do that this firm can't run without you. Become indispensable." Spectacular advice. Awareness precedes choice which precedes results. As you learn what the best do, you will develop new awareness. With better awareness, you will make better choices. And with better choices, you are certain to see better results. Investing in learning and getting your skills to world class is the smartest investment you'll ever make. Master your craft and you'll get to greatness.

Please don't tell me you are too busy to spend at least 60 minutes a day learning. Some of the busiest people I know read or listen to CDs or do online training for at least an hour a day.

A lot of people are too busy being busy. Shift from being busy to getting results. At robinsharma.com, you will find a rich source of resources to help you become a lifelong learner, including my blog, free podcasts, a listing of my favorite books, and a wealth of other knowledge tools to speed you to your best.

Investing in learning and getting your skill to world class is the smartest investment you'll ever make.

So take the first step today. Rather than watching TV tonight, make the time to read. Learn what the superstars in your profession do to stay on top. Learn how to create greater wellness in your life. Learn how to master your time. Learn how to live your highest life.

74

See Through the Eyes of Understanding

The sad fact is that so many people look for the worst in others. They see them through the eyes of their own anger, fear and limitation. If someone shows up late for a meeting, they impute a negative intent to that person, saying, "They are so rude." If someone makes a mistake on an expense report, they grumble, "That person is so dishonest." If someone miscommunicates a point, they silently say, "She's a liar." Real leaders are different. They look for the best in people. Jack Welch, the former CEO of GE, said it so well: "The most important job you have is growing your people, giving them a chance to reach their dreams."

I want to be clear. I'm not suggesting that leaders avoid reality. Not at all. They make the hard calls when they need to. I've mentioned in an earlier chapter that the best don't worry about being liked—they just do what their conscience tells them is right. What I'm really saying is that the best leaders see through the eyes of understanding. If someone is late, they try to get to the truth. Maybe there's a time management problem to coach around or a sick child to help. An error on an expense account could be the result of a poor process in place or the employee's disorganization. The miscommunication might be all about the person communicating having weak skills in this area—an opportunity for improvement.

Today, rather than looking for the worst in people, I encourage you to look for what's best within them. Sure some people really are inconsiderate or dishonest or uncaring. But in my experience—and I've worked with a lot of people over the years—most people are good. Few human beings wake up in the morning and ask themselves: "What can I do today to mess up someone else's day or undermine my credibility or ruin our business?" Most of the mistakes people make are the result of a lack of awareness. Most people just don't know better—so stop taking it so personally.

> # Few human beings wake up in the morning and ask themselves: "What can I do today to mess up someone else's day or undermine my credibility or ruin our business?"

And here's the payoff for you: As you seek out the good in people, not only will they want to show up more fully for you, but you will see more good in your world.

75

The Heart of Your House

Every great business has a clearly articulated business model and strategic plan. That's all about the design and focus of the business. But so few people have taken the time to design their own lives. If you don't know where you are going, then how will you know when you get there? And how can you hit a target you can't even see?

In the hotel industry, there's a name for all the stuff that goes on behind the scenes that guests don't see. All the things that need to unfold in accounting, in housekeeping, in the kitchen and in the laundry that are mission-critical yet not public. All those activities are called "the heart of the house." When "the heart of the house" is in superb order and operating with near-flawless execution, the same will hold true for the external guest experience.

Do you have a "business model" for your life? Do you have a strategic plan for your dreams?

Here's the big idea for you: To get to your best life, I suggest you ensure the heart of your house is nice and tidy. Do you have a "business model" for your life? Do you have a strategic plan for your dreams? Have you recorded your most closely cherished values and your life's most important priorities on a piece of paper, which you then review every morning to keep you locked onto what's most important? These are all aspects of "the heart of the house," your internal operations process that will direct and govern your external results.

Sure it takes time to do this inner work. And sure we all have a ton of urgent things we need to do right now. But there's no point in being busy if you're busy doing the wrong things.

76

Become an Inspirational Human Being

I dropped my son off at school the other day and was amused by what he did when he walked into his classroom. He passed one of his buddies and said: "Why so glum, chum?" His friend, who had been looking very serious, looked up. Both kids broke into laughter. Got me smiling. Then it got me thinking.

Greatness in business as well as in life comes by being an inspirational human being. We need to uplift people by our attitude and our very presence. When we see someone feeling down or experiencing a struggle or doubting their potential or in need of a kind word, it's our duty to help them, perhaps by asking, "Why so glum, chum?"

The best way to lead and elevate another human being—whether that means a co-worker or a family member or a friend—is to model the behavior you wish to see. The best way to influence others is to lead by example. You can preach a better sermon with your life than with your words. Talk really is cheap. Extraordinary human beings live their message. They walk their talk. And above all else, they are inspirational. Are you?

One of the nicest compliments I've ever received was from a woman who came up to me after a keynote speech I gave to 2000 fitness professionals for a great organization called Can-Fit-Pro. "Robin, I loved your presentation," she said, full of emotion. I asked why. "I'm not really sure. I guess you just inspired me to be a better human being." What would the organizations we work for and the communities we live in and the planet we walk on look like if each and every one of us did our part to be inspirational leaders each day—encouraging them to be better human beings? We can curse the darkness or we can light a candle. And our world needs more light. Shine. Today.

Greatness in business as well as in life comes by being an inspirational human being.

77

Make a Dent in the Universe

I'm up earlier than usual as I write this chapter. Listened to some beautiful music that is part chillout and part Indian. I wrote in my journal a bit. Wrote about how much I love my children. Wrote about where my life's at. Wrote about where I want to take it. And I wrote about my hunger to have an impact. Leadership—as a human being—is about having an impact. Making a difference. Leaving things better than you found them.

When I met Shimon Peres, I asked him what he believed the purpose of life to be. He replied without hesitation: "To find a cause that's larger than yourself and then to give your life to it." What would this world of ours look like if each of us had found our cause or life's purpose and were then passionately pursuing it? There would be less hatred, fewer wars and more love. And we'd be united as one race. As Coretta Scott King said: "When you are willing to make sacrifices for a great cause, you will never be alone."

Apple CEO Steve Jobs used to tell his people that by showing up at their best they would have the opportunity to "make a dent in the universe." Jobs definitely gets it. Sure it's important to make a profit in business. Sure you want your enterprise to be operationally excellent. Sure you want high-quality products

and services. And sure you need to keep innovating and growing your brand. But isn't having an impact in the world—by
helping your clients and positively influencing others—what
business is ultimately about?

Isn't having an **impact** in the world—
by helping your clients and positively
influencing others—what business
is **ultimately** about?

So a gentle question from a man who wishes only the best
for you: "What dent will you make today?" What cause will you
pursue? What contribution will you make—at work, at home—
in life?

78

Not All Leaders Are the Same

Many executives come up to me after presentations and ask me about my statement "Everyone needs to be a leader." As I've suggested, in my leadership seminars, I always make the point that for a company to get to greatness, every person on the team needs to see himself or herself as a leader. The best companies on the planet grow leaders and develop leadership potential throughout the organization faster than their competition. Making that happen is their number-one focus. And they do it quickly. I said that earlier, but it's worth repeating.

Everyone is a leader. But not everyone is the same.

But I'm not saying everyone should run the company. That makes no sense. Everyone is a leader but not everyone does the same thing. Here's a metaphor to drive the distinction home for you. I love U2. Bono is the lead singer. Larry Mullen Jr. is the drummer. Chaos would ensue if Larry tried to be the lead singer and Bono got confused and started playing the drums.

Or imagine if the tour manager thought he could be Bono for a night and walked on stage to do so while Bono was in his dressing room. Not good.

Know your role. Everyone needs to behave like a leader—no matter what they do. Everyone needs to demonstrate leadership traits—regardless of their position. That means everyone needs to take responsibility for getting the results that they generate. Everyone needs to do their part to shape culture. Everyone needs to be positive and inspirational. Everyone needs to keep customers happy and protect the brand. Everyone is a leader. But not everyone is the same.

Six Reasons to Set Goals

I know what you're thinking: "Robin, give me a topic that's fresh and original and challenging. Why are you writing about goals? We know this stuff. It's boring!" Few success practices are as important as articulating your most closely held goals and then reviewing them daily. Getting masterful at setting and then considering your goals on a consistent basis is essential to a life of greatness. And yet, guess what? Most people don't spend more than an hour a year doing this. It's true: People spend more time planning their summer vacations than they do designing their lives.

In my mind, there are six big reasons for you to set goals: Focus, Growth, Intentionality, Measurement, Alignment and Inspiration.

FOCUS. *Where your focus goes your energy flows. I feel so very blessed to be the success coach to some genuine superstars in the field of business. Billionaires, celebrity entrepreneurs, captains of industry. One of their primary traits of greatness is their focus. They know their "vital few," in other words, the key goals they need to achieve to get to the extraordinary. And then they focus like crazy on them. Goals breed focus. Simple but powerful idea.*

GROWTH. *Goal-setting promotes personal growth. The real value of reaching a goal lies not in the result achieved but in what the journey you've walked to get to the goal has made of you as a person.*

INTENTIONALITY. *It's easy to live life by accident and sleepwalk through your days. If you don't act on life, life has a way of acting on you. By articulating your goals and then reviewing them for five minutes each morning, you will exert your influence on life and live in a proactive rather than reactive manner. By setting goals, you will have a framework or decision matrix that will drive better choices. You will become aware—within a few seconds—when you get off plan. You'll make fewer mistakes and get more done in less time. As the novelist Saul Bellow said: "A plan relieves you of the torment of choice."*

Setting your goals is a **bold** play for your best life. Setting your goals is an act of **heroism** because you are reaching for the potential that has been **invested** in you.

MEASUREMENT. *One of our corporate clients is El Al, Israel's national airline. We did some leadership training for its management team. Amos Shapiro, the CEO who ran the airline, offered me a tour of Tel Aviv's spectacular airport when I was last there. In one of the meeting rooms used by his staff, a statement appeared on a crumpled piece of paper stuck to a wall: "What gets measured gets improved." Big thought. Setting goals gives you something to measure. If your physical goal is* to get down to 12% body fat, you have a standard against which to measure your progress. And as you measure, you have a basis on which to improve. With a clearer awareness of your goals you can make better choices. With better choices, you will see better results.

ALIGNMENT. *I'll share one of my best "secrets of success" with you: Ensure your daily actions are aligned with your deepest values. Let me put it another way: There can be no happiness if your commitments are not congruent with your convictions. Isn't that what integrity is all about, ensuring that your schedule reflects your values and what you stand for? Setting clear goals that are aligned with your most important values is a superb way to get to personal greatness.*

INSPIRATION. *Goals breathe life into your days. The very act of articulating your goals on a crisp white piece of paper causes you to step into a whole new possibility for what your life can become. Setting your goals is a statement that you refuse to be ordinary. Setting your goals is a bold play for your best life. Setting your goals is an act of heroism because you are reaching for the potential that has been invested in you. As Mark Twain noted: "If everyone was satisfied with themselves there would be no heroes."*

80

Remember the Boomerang Effect

Big idea: the very thing you most want to see more of in your life is the very thing you need to give away.

Want more credit for all you do and who you are? Be the one who gives credit to others. Spread it like wildfire. Give away what you most want. This will create a space in the minds and hearts of all those around you to give more credit.

Give out what you most want to come back.

Want more understanding from others? Be more understanding and give that out.

Want more loyalty? Be the most loyal person you know. Watch what happens.

Want more love? Give more love.

I believe life wants you to win. Most people just get in their own way and sabotage their success. They let their fears keep them from greatness. They let their limitations become their chains. They become their own worst enemies. To get all that life wants for you, apply what I call the Boomerang Effect: Give out what you most want to see come back. It's a gorgeous life you have in store for you. Just go out and get it.

81

Make People Feel Good

People do business with people who make them feel good. Human beings are creatures of emotion. We want to be with those who make us feel happy and special and cared for and safe.

There are two people I want to introduce you to: a farmer named Steve and Jake the variety store owner, two people who know more about business-building than most CEOs. Steve sells pumpkins. I live in Canada, and every autumn the kids and I hop into our car and drive half an hour to get our Halloween pumpkins from this farmer who never seems to grow older. Sure we could get our pumpkins from the local grocery store five minutes from our home. But then we'd miss the feelings that Steve generates within us. He remembers our names. He makes us laugh. He tells us stories. He reminds us of what's best in the world (farmers are good at that). And we drive away with a big batch of pumpkins and joy in our hearts. By the way, Steve's business is unbelievably successful.

Next comes Jake. Jake runs a variety store. When the kids and I go in, he greets us by name. He knows our birthdays (records them in a little black book). Jake orders magazines like *Dwell*, *Azure* and *Business 2.0* especially for me (no extra charge, of course). His manners are flawless. He always smiles. He makes us feel good. There are at least five other corner stores in our neighborhood, but Jake is a master at relationship-building. So he has our loyalty. Oh, and the guy's a millionaire.

Being good is being wise. It's a smart business strategy. So be like Steve. Model Jake. Make people feel good about doing business with you. You'll lead the field. You'll have fun doing it. And it's just the right thing to do.

"Do good and leave behind a virtue that the storm of time can never destroy."

Makes me think of the words etched on a slip of paper one seminar participant handed to me after an event a few months ago that read simply: "Do good and leave behind a virtue that the storm of time can never destroy." I asked him who authored those words. His reply was brief: "The wisest person I've ever known—my grandfather."

82

Commit to First Class

One of the personal habits I've consistently observed in the star performers and extraordinary leaders I've coached is their commitment to ensuring that their surroundings reflect their devotion to being world class. They drive the highest quality cars, live in the best homes and wear the finest clothes. Their philosophy generally seems to be, "I stand for being the best so it only makes sense that I should invest in the best." Now here's the big idea: They held that belief even when they were not successful.

Greatness is, above all else, a state of mind. You need to believe in your potential and power before you can bring them to life. You need to *feel* like you are extraordinary before you can become extraordinary. I call this "emotional blueprinting." To see spectacular results in your external life, you have to emotionally—viscerally—create a blueprint of your vision within your inner life.

One of the best ways I've discovered to achieve this feeling is to ensure that everything you surround yourself with is at the highest level. I remember reading a book years ago, written by a magician named Al Koran, called *Bring Out the Magic in Your Mind*. One of the ideas that stayed with me is his suggestion that, in order to be successful, it's important to go where the successful people are. Even if you have only $10, go have a coffee at the best restaurant in your city. His point? Your surroundings shape the way you feel. And the way you feel drives what you do. Feel world class and you'll behave world class.

Rewarding yourself with good things sends a message to the deepest—and highest—part of you. One that says "I'm worth it—and I deserve it."

Invest in the best. Buy the highest quality goods you can possibly afford. Better to buy one superb pair of shoes than three cheap ones (they'll last you longer and make you feel great while you are wearing them). I love the line: "Quality is remembered long after price is forgotten." So true. When I was a young lawyer, just starting out, I took part of my first paycheck and invested it in a great watch. It wasn't a Rolex or a Cartier. But it was a good one—the best I could afford. My thinking was that it would last for years, make me feel successful while I wore it and actually end up saving me money because it would rarely need repairs. One of my friends, who always looked for the cheapest deal, laughed at me. But I turned out to be right (that does happen to me from time to time). My watch is still working perfectly. Never needed even one repair. My friend has gone through six watches during this time. Not only has he denied himself the positive feelings that high quality would have brought, but he has actually ended up spending more money than I did. Missed the forest for the trees.

I'm in no way encouraging a senseless addiction to material things. All I'm saying is that if you're really serious about standing for the best (and I know you are), then surround yourself with the best. Rewarding yourself with good things sends a message to the deepest—and highest—part of you. One that says "I'm worth it—and I deserve it." One that will inspire you to reach even higher, work even harder and be even better. To anyone who says that our self-worth should be so strong that high-quality goods won't affect how we feel, I'd respectfully suggest that such a statement misses the reality of human nature. I'm one of the most idealistic people you'll ever meet. But I'm also a realist ("in all things balance," observed the Buddha). Every one of us likes nice things. They bring us pleasure. They appeal to our senses, just like a beautiful sunset or a magnificent mountain. True, material possessions don't bring lasting happiness. And there are many things in life that are far more important. But such things still are important.

The best invest in the best. I might not be popular with you for making this point. But I owe you my truth. Reminds me of the words of one of my clients: "My tastes are simple—I just want the best."

83

Do a Clean Sweep

I've spent much of the past twelve months in what I call Strategic Hibernation—pulling back from much of the "busyness" of my life and rethinking things like my priorities, my values and my personal philosophy. I've accepted fewer social invitations, limited many activities and spent a lot more time in reflection—just to make certain I'm climbing the right mountain and spending my days in the way they should be spent. I've also spent a lot of time this year doing a "Clean Sweep."

A Clean Sweep is a superb way to streamline, simplify and refocus your life. Most of us have a ton of baggage and clutter that we carry with us on this journey. These might include "messes," like incomplete relationships or people you have yet to forgive (or apologize to). The baggage in your life could include "undones," like a will that needs to be prepared or a life insurance policy that should be updated. The clutter could relate to an unkempt yard or a bunch of unpacked boxes stacked in a spare room. The powerful idea is this: When you Clean Sweep these things—put them into order or delete what needs to be eliminated from your life—you will feel lighter, happier and your mind will experience more peace.

My Clean Sweep involved getting a will, getting rid of a lot of things I hadn't used for a while, putting a financial plan in place, tidying up my physical spaces, saying goodbye to pursuits that were not aligned with my personal and professional strategic objectives (goals), installing systems to be more efficient and spending a lot of time refining the model of my business. Guess what? It worked—beautifully.

Delete what needs to be eliminated from your life—you will feel lighter, happier and your mind will experience more peace.

I have more time to do what's most important. I'm more relaxed and in the flow. I have more energy (messes—whether physical or emotional—drain you). I am more creative. And I'm having more fun. So do a Clean Sweep of your life. And start soon. The results just might astonish you.

84

Follow the Million Dollar Baby Rule

I loved the film *Million Dollar Baby*. Deeply moving. Unforgettable. And though it was rich with so many life lessons, there's one in particular that I still think about: "Protect yourself."

I believe I'm a world-class optimist. I try to stay incredibly positive. I'm committed to seeing the best in every situation, and the good in every person I meet. I really do expect the best from life. But I also prepare for the worst. That just makes sense to me. Life's not a fairy tale. I must say that expecting the best but preparing for the worst is not an easy balancing act. But I think it's an important one for us to work on and get right as we reach for our own unique forms of personal greatness.

So be splendidly loving and kind to people. Definitely. Give of yourself and help all those around you as much as you can. Undoubtedly. Be one of those special people who leaves people better than you found them. But I also suggest that you not become a martyr. The thing about martyrs is that most of them get burned at the stake. Balance being kind and considerate to others with being kind and considerate to yourself. Balance giving away your energy inspiring others with replenishing your energy so you remain inspired yourself. Strike that delicate balance between loving others and loving yourself.

The thing about **martyrs** is that most of them get **burned** at the stake.

Set boundaries. Know your limits. Don't go to extremes. Protect yourself.

85

The Earth Is Small

Lots of our clients are talking about Thomas Friedman's book *The Earth Is Flat*. It's all about globalization and a leveling of the playing field by emerging economies. Excellent book. The title made me think about a totally different topic, though: the value of perspective.

The world isn't flat—the world is small. Here's the point I'm trying to offer to you: We live on a small planet in a gigantic universe. Stephen Hawking, the famed physicist, said that we are on a minor planet of a very average star in the outer suburb of one of a hundred billion galaxies. And you and I are just one of billions of people here. Are the problems we face as we walk through our days really so big? A little dose of perspective makes life easier to manage.

A question I sometimes ask myself when I'm facing a struggle is this one: "Will this matter a year from now?" If not, I move on—fast. Another great question I invite you to share with your team at work or your family at home is: "Has someone died here?" If not, things settle down and calmer minds generally prevail.

Keep perspective. Most of the problems we think are disasters turn out to be blessings, in hindsight. I've faced things in my life that seemed so painful at first. Thought the world would end. But with the passage of time, those evolved into the very things that made my life better and happier and more reward-ing. And my guess is that the same holds true for you.

Life is **short,** and the world is small—but it's really, really **wide.**

So do some inner work around perspective today. Focus on the good. Smile and laugh more. Life is short, and the world is small—but it's also really, really wide.

86

Guests Are God

I've learned some of the deepest lessons on life from guys driving taxis. Want some big-time wisdom? Jump in a cab. Put away your Blackberry or your cell phone and get to know the human being in front of you. He speaks to hundreds of people each day. Very often, he's wiser than you could imagine. I was reminded of that last night.

I'm in Mumbai as I write this chapter. Here to give a day-long leadership seminar and then do another presentation for the Young Presidents' Organization tonight. I love this place. Love the food. Love the energy. Love the people. The driver's name was Ramesh Sharma. He saw my name on the taxi reservation sheet. "Robin Sharma . . . where's your father from?" We started a long chat (Mumbai traffic is crazy—we had lots of time) and really connected. He laughed like a child—Indians are among the happiest people I've met anywhere in the world. He told me about his family, his passion for reading, his philosophy. And then he said something I'll never forget.

"In the North of India, where I'm from," he noted with pride, "a guest is God. When someone comes to our home, we treat them with the highest of respect and love. Even if we have to miss eating, we make sure they are well fed. That's our culture. It brings us joy." Brilliant.

In your life, and in your organization, do you treat your "guests like gods"? Is that idea a part of your personal and organizational culture? And let me also ask you: What would your personal life look like if everyone who visited you and intersected the journey of your days was treated like a god (whether that person was a family member or a stranger on the street)? What would your professional life look like if you treated your customers with reverence and admiration? You'd be world class. You'd be more successful. You'd be happier. You'd get to greatness.

In your life, and in your organization, do you treat your "guests like Gods"?

So leave work 30 minutes earlier today. Hop into a cab and go for a ride. Don't bring a newspaper or a phone. Just bring an open mind (and a pen). And get to know the human in the car with you. You might love what you hear.

87

The Beauty of Time

Time is a beautiful commodity. It is part of the hardware of life. What you do with it shapes, in so many ways, what your life looks like. And yet, while almost every one of us wishes for more time, we misuse the time we have.

I'm no guru, you know that. But I've become pretty good at using my time well. Time wasted is time lost and the big idea on time is that once it's lost, it can never be regained.

The big idea on time is that once it's lost, it can never be regained.

I recently read that John Templeton, the celebrated financier, never went anywhere without a book in his briefcase. This way, if he found himself in a long line, he could use the downtime to read, learn and grow. I also read in *Rolling Stone* that Madonna hates wasting time. She used to bring a book with her when she'd go out to a nightclub to use the time when she wasn't dancing efficiently. My coaching clients are like that. And they lead big lives as a result of that giant devotion to time management.

I want to be clear: I'm in no way suggesting that every minute of your days, weeks and months need to be scheduled. Be spontaneous. Be playful. Be free. I'm a free spirit at heart. I just find that the people who have the most time for fun are those who know how to plan and then use their time well. In my experience, the people who feel stress the most and lead their lives like a five-alarm fire are those who leave life to chance and make no time to set schedules, articulate goals and follow well-thought-out plans. "Anxiety is caused by a lack of control, organization, preparation and action," observed thinker David Kekich. Powerful thought.

88

On Mountains and Mastering Change

Just met a reader at a book signing. He was a cynic—even after he read one of my books. No worries—not everyone is open to my words. And I have no need to be right. I just share the philosophy that feels truthful to me. If someone doesn't agree with it—well, not everyone likes coffee either. Diversity of opinion is what makes life so interesting. This reader was kind though. Said he actually loved the book; he just didn't believe it would help him. Hmmm.

Faith and belief do move mountains. And if you don't believe that an idea will work, then there's no chance you'll act on it (and if you don't act, how can you get results?). Thought is the mother of action and your beliefs really do become self-fulfilling prophecies.

I thought a lot about the reader's comments after the book signing. If I had the chance to meet him again, I'd use the metaphor of mountain-climbing to help him understand that people truly can make changes that last. I'll offer my thinking on this point to you. I have three thoughts, in particular, to help you take the ideas I've shared so far in *The Greatness Guide* and integrate them into your life so that you see real and lasting results:

DEFINE WHAT THE MOUNTAINTOP LOOKS LIKE. *I suggest you articulate, in writing, what success looks like to you. Note what needs to change in your life for you to feel spectacularly successful and what will happen if you don't improve. Then record your goals for all the key areas of your life. Write out what you want your reality to appear as five years from now. List the values you want to stand for. Clarity precedes success—and awareness precedes transformation.*

START CLIMBING. *There's great power in starting (I call it the Power of a Start). A single act—done now—sets forces into play. It generates momentum. And with the action you begin to experience positive results. That begins a positive feedback loop: more action, more results. And that, in turn, promotes confidence.*

You can't get to the **top** of Everest by jumping up the mountain. You get to the mountaintop by taking **incremental** steps. Step by step you get to the goal.

TAKE SMALL STEPS. *You can't get to the top of Everest by jumping up the mountain. You get to the mountaintop by taking incremental steps. Step by step you get to the goal. Every step gets you closer to the dream. Life's like that too. Small steps each day get you to greatness over* *time. Why? Because the days really do become weeks and weeks become months and months become years. You'll get to the end of your life any-way—why not reach that place as an extraordinary human being?*

89

What Happened to "Please"?

I was just in Starbucks getting a soy latte (love it with brown sugar). The woman next to me collects her coffee from the barista and then says: "Can I have a tray?" She didn't say it rudely—she just wasn't polite. That got me thinking. Whatever happened to "please"?

To me, "please" means "I respect you." "Thank you" means "I appreciate you." Good manners are powerful in showing those around you that you care about them. I love Frankie Byrne's line that "respect is love in plain clothes." How often have you bought something at a store or ordered something in a restaurant and just ached to hear some good manners?

Authentic success is not complicated. It comes down to consistently following a series of fundamentals. Those who get to greatness just run the basics—bit by bit, day by day—over many months and years. It's not hard at all. It just takes small acts of daily discipline around a few important things. But when done over time—amazing results appear. The best among us just do the things most of us already know we should do to live an extraordinary life really well. And they do it consistently. One of the key things they do is say "please" a lot.

Good manners are a stepping stone to being a remarkable human being, whether as a mother, a father, a salesperson or the CEO. They really do show people that you respect them. Yes, having good manners is common sense. But as the French philosopher Voltaire once said: "Common sense is anything but common." And if all this stuff is so obvious, how come most people don't do it?

Good manners are a stepping stone to being a remarkable human being.

90

Bon Jovi and the Power of Focus

Someone told me a while ago that Jon Bon Jovi is a fan of *The Monk Who Sold His Ferrari*. Interesting. I've always admired the man for his passion and his music. This morning I heard a song of his in which he sings: "When the world gets in my face, I say have a nice day." Got me thinking about Bon Jovi, his long career and why he's still going strong after so many years.

There's great power in focusing on what you want. Seems like such an obvious statement, yet most of us miss it. Dreams can come true. You can get to a place called Extraordinary in your career. You can find love deeper than you've ever imagined. You can realize world-class vitality and find lasting fulfillment. But you need to focus. The person who tries to do everything accomplishes nothing. Most people try to be all things to everyone. And so they end up nothing to anyone. Confucius nailed the point: "Person who chases two rabbits catches neither." Big idea.

What you focus on grows. What you concentrate on is what you see more of in your life. Think about that line. Focus on financial mastery and you'll see your economic life improve.

Focus on being more loving and your relationships will improve. Focus on your physical dimension by exercising and following a superb diet and your health will improve. Focus. Focus. Focus. That's what the best of the best do. Tunnel vision around their biggest To Do's. They stick to their knitting rather than scattering their brilliance. A few months ago I had dinner with a billionaire client of mine. I asked him what was the single best thing he did to get to his financial mastery. "I made this goal my sole reference point," came the instant reply.

The person who tries to do everything accomplishes nothing.

Back to Jon Bon Jovi. From what I can tell, he's still around and doing great because he had an idea about what his music would be and where he could take it, and then he stayed focused on that mission. I've heard he's faced some tough times (join the club). But he didn't give up. He didn't play victim. He remained strong and on course. He stayed true to his fans and himself.

91

Do a "101 Things to Do Before I Die" List

This is a powerful idea. Got it from an article I read on Ted Leonsis, vice-chairman of AOL. A number of years ago he was on an airplane that looked like it was going to crash. It didn't, but the brush with death changed the way he viewed life—and lived it. He decided, as soon as he got off the plane, to live with a greater sense of passion, purpose and urgency. So he took out a piece of paper and scribbled out a list of the 101 things he was absolutely committed to doing before he died. Borrowing from his example, I've done the same. It has worked wonders.

It never ceases to amaze me how powerful a practice written goal-setting is. Just ask anyone who does it on a consistent basis. Leonsis, whose list included everything from starting a family to owning a professional sports franchise, has accomplished two-thirds of the objectives he wrote down. Clarity clearly does precede success. And with heightened awareness of what's most important comes wiser choices.

As for me, I'm still in hot pursuit of my dreams. But so many of the goals on my list have been achieved, including starting a charity to help disadvantaged children become leaders, watching the sun set on the tiny Greek island of Santorini and showing my kids Michelangelo's statue *David*. And I'm just getting started. So should you.

He took out a piece of paper and scribbled out a list of the 101 things he was absolutely **committed** to doing before he died.

92

Spend Time with Your Kids

At the end of our lives, few of us regret not having made more money. Just doesn't happen. What we truly regret are the places we didn't visit, the friendships we didn't nurture, the risks we didn't take and the things we didn't do with the people we love. Brings me to the point I need to passionately make: Spend time with your kids.

I love what I do. Sure there are lots of airplanes (I still feel like a kid on every flight takeoff). Lots of big events in cool places. Lots of great conversations with interesting people from all walks of life. Lots of wonderful opportunities to share my message with those who need it. But nothing—and I really do mean nothing—is more important to me than being a great dad. I've worked with too many executives who get to the top of the mountain and realized that they lost what mattered most along the way.

It's human nature to take the people who love us the most for granted. I'm not saying that's a good thing—I'm saying that's just the way we are wired. We need to resist our nature and develop a rich sense of gratitude for our family. Don't be one of those people who has to experience loss (through divorce or death) before you wake up to the blessings you have. I've seen that happen. All the time. With people all around the world.

If you had 30 minutes left to live, you'd be reaching for your phone to tell those closest to you how much you love them. Then you'd run home and, holding your heart in your hand, speak truthfully about the love that you feel. Just think about the tragedy of 9/11. I still remember those cell phone calls from the people trapped in the towers. Heartbreaking.

If you had 30 minutes left to live, you'd be reaching for your phone to tell those closest to you how much you love them.

I know you're busy. Tons to do. Places to go and people to meet. But take a minute, right here and right now to make a call. Tell your kids how much you care. Tell your wife or your husband or your mom or your dad or your brother or sister or best friend how you feel about them. You'll never regret it. Trust me.

93

Get Goofy at Work

What's the point of doing something if you're not having fun? Life's just too short to be miserable all the time, wouldn't you agree? The best organizations are fun places to be. Sure they demand excellent performance, relentless innovation and superb execution around deliverables. But they also promote fun. Being happy—and laughing—at work promotes collaboration, creativity and commitment. The company that plays together stays together. And fun is good for the bottom line because people love doing business with people who love doing business.

Life's just **too short** to be miserable.

Now let's talk about your personal life. Having any fun? In my twenties and thirties, I was serious. Mr. Serious. "The purpose of life is a life of purpose" was my driving belief. I wanted to change the world and servant leadership was the name of the game. I worked hard and played little. Only recently did I have a big "a-ha" around the value of fun as I journey through life. I'm different now. I've still got my eye on the mountaintop, but I've become much more attentive to enjoying the climb. I get goofy with my kids constantly. I ski with my friends. I'll add a day to a business trip to visit an art gallery as I did a few weeks ago while I was in London. Because having a good time makes life far better. And a lot more fun.

94

Revere Great Design

I'm back at the Frankfurt airport as I write this chapter. Being here in Germany, I can't help noticing that design matters in this country. The hand towel dispensers in the bathrooms work flawlessly and are ingenious. The latte machines in the lounge read my mind. Luggage carts are not only functional—they are beautiful. The Germans get it—design matters.

Ford has repositioned itself as a design firm that sells cars. Love it. In this world where consumers have more choice than ever, good design is one of the best ways for you, your products and your organization to pop out of the crowd and grab attention. Look at Apple's iPod, one of the sexiest gadgets you'll ever feast your eyes on (I wouldn't dream of traveling without mine). Sure, keeping 10,000 songs in your back pocket is fantastic. But the design is what made us fall in love with it. Look at Apple's iBook. Actually, look at almost anything that creative and bold company does and you'll see what world class looks like when it comes to design.

Do a Google search for Philippe Starck, a genius of design. Look what he did with partner Ian Schrager to create the boutique hotel category over a decade ago and make people's jaws drop when they entered their hotels. (St. Martin's Lane in London and The Hudson in New York are still two of my favorite places to sleep.) That's what good design does. Or invest in a Bodum French Press coffee maker. Makes super java. Looks great in my kitchen. Its great design has inspired me to tell everyone I know about it. Superb design creates product evangelists. "Businesspeople don't need to understand designers better. They need to be designers," noted Roger Martin, dean of The Rotman Management School in Toronto.

"Businesspeople don't need to understand designers better. They need to be designers."

Here's a powerful thought for you to take away: Human beings need mystery to be happy in life. If life is bland, we experience no joy. Good design adds to that mystery. It makes life interesting. It connects with the artist that resides within each of us. It surprises us. And isn't surprising people one of the main aims of being in business and crafting an extraordinary life?

95

On Evian Water and You as a Big-Time Dreamer

If people don't laugh at you and your ideas at least once a week, you're not pushing the envelope.

There, I said it. Needed to. I'm tired of seeing boring businesses and people afraid to take the road less traveled. Most of the things that fill us with fear never happen, so why let them keep you small?

Great people run toward their resistances and play out on the edges of their lives. And great companies spend far less time benchmarking others than creating new ways of delivering outrageous value to their customers. Why? Because the world doesn't need a better clone. We don't need more copycats. The world needs more human beings and enterprises that make us say wow. That rock our worlds. The world needs more giant ideas that no one's thought of to enrich our customers and improve our communities and elevate the planet. The world needs more visionaries, dreamers and outright revolutionaries. I love what Tom Chappell, founder of Tom's of Maine, said: "Success means never letting the competition define you. Instead, you have to

define yourself based on a point of view you care deeply about."
Beautiful.

One client recently shared that he thought it was daring
for me and my team to have a picture on our rebranded website of me with my eyes closed, holding a dove. "What would all
your corporate clients, like Microsoft, IBM, Nike and FedEx,
think of it?" he asked. "Those companies stand for reinvention
and innovation," I replied. "I think they'd applaud the bold
move." The designer of the new multimedia show I'm running
at my presentations shared that the colors I'd chosen were risky
because they were not "standard corporate colors." "Thanks for
the compliment," I joked. Business needs more daring. Business needs more people willing to take risks and play out on
the skinny branches. Business needs more human beings like
Richard Branson and his devotion to putting tourists into space
with his company Virgin Galactic. I love people like that. They
inspire me.

Business needs more daring. Business needs more people willing to take risks and play out on the skinny branches.

All innovators are initially laughed at. Just the way it is.
They laughed at Columbus when he said the earth was round.
They laughed at the Wright Brothers, who vowed a human being
could fly. They laughed at the guys at RIM when they launched
the BlackBerry. They laughed at the founder of Evian, who
believed people would pay money for water. Who's laughing

now? I guess the universe really does favor the brave.

People pay for originality (big idea there). You want to lead the field in your business? Be different. Let them laugh. Let them call you crazy. Let them snicker. Stay true to your vision. Dream bigger. Don't be ordinary. It's the kiss of death, as far as I can tell.

96

Be like Garth

Throughout this book I've encouraged you to "lead without title," to show up fully and to make a difference. There's a man who lived the philosophy I evangelize. His name was Garth Taylor. He died recently. I want to honor him.

Dr. Garth Alfred Taylor was born in Montego Bay, Jamaica, in 1944. He was a gifted eye surgeon, a family man and—above all else—a humanitarian. One of his favorite sayings was: "I came into this world with nothing, and all I'm going to leave with is my conscience." My guess is he did.

Dr. Taylor first came to my attention through my brother Sanjay, a gifted eye surgeon in his own right. Garth was a colleague of Sanjay's, and a fan of my books. So I signed a few for him one morning and sent them off. I heard it made him very happy.

What made Garth's impact so profound was that he didn't just practice medicine—he lived it. For more than 20 years, he traveled around the world, to developing nations, selflessly helping to save people's sight. In his own words: "I found my nirvana 23 years ago . . . by treating avoidable blindness. People don't just get back their sight, they get back their self-esteem." Because he cared—and had the courage to act—he blessed the lives of thousands of people. Sanjay attended

Dr. Taylor's funeral. The church was so full many people had to stand out on the street.

"I came into this world with **nothing,** and all I'm going to leave with is my **conscience."**

As you near the end of *The Greatness Guide* and our time together, I invite you to think about the truths I've respectfully shared. Reflect on what you want to stand for and what will be your impact. And then contemplate the words of Dr. Garth Taylor: "Until I have no breath to breathe, I will continue to do this because I think I was chosen for this, not for money, not for compensation but just to make the quality of life of my fellow human beings better."

97

Don't Give Up

I'm sitting here in my study as I write, drinking coffee, and thinking. Not daydreaming. Not wasting time. Not worrying. Simply thinking. One of my best habits. Mostly I'm thinking about the importance of having a sense of mission and then staying true to it. It's not easy though.

I've found that the bigger I dream, the more obstacles I face. My mission in life is pretty straightforward: I want to help human beings become extraordinary and organizations get to world class. I have such passion to realize that dream and do my part to make this world a better place. This isn't just a business to me—it's my calling. But the higher I reach, the more I get tested. Sound familiar?

But challenges are good. We grow through them. We are most alive amidst danger. Papa Wallenda—the great high-wire walker—said it so well: "Life is lived out on the wire. The rest is just waiting." The wisest among us—the genuine leaders—smile in the face of adversity. They understand that life tests the big dreamers—the passionate revolutionaries. It's almost like a weeding-out process—only the strong (and the best) get to live their heartsong. I really love what Amazon.com founder Jeff Bezos once said: "I knew that if I failed I wouldn't regret that, but I knew the one thing I might regret is not trying."

So I'll rise above any resistance I meet. I'll keep my eyes on the dream. I'll stay on message and solidly on mission. Because this world belongs to us dreamers—you and me. And whether we ultimately win or not, we will have made a difference. And that's good enough for me.

Life tests the big dreamers—the passionate revolutionaries.

Get Big on Self-Care

Leadership begins within. Organizational leadership begins with personal leadership. You can't be great at work until you feel great. You can't make someone feel good about themselves until you feel good about yourself. You can't be a source of positive energy if you have no energy. The doorway to success swings outward—not inward.

Organizational leadership begins with **personal** leadership. You can't be great at work until you feel **great**.

On your next flight, listen to the flight attendant. "Put the oxygen mask on your own mouth before you try to help anyone else." The logic is clear: If you can't breathe, you are useless to those around you. Nice metaphor for personal leadership. Make the time to care for yourself. Get into great shape. Read good business books and inspiring autobiographies. Plan and improve your skills. Work with a coach. Spend excellent time with loved ones. Commune with nature. Enjoy life while you chase success.

By caring for yourself, you will be able to give more to others. By ensuring that you are on your best game, your leadership effectiveness will be guaranteed. And by making the time to enjoy life, you'll be more enjoyable to be around.

Guess Who Inspires Me?

At a booksigning the other day a man stood up and asked: "Robin, what keeps you going? What is the source of your energy? Who inspires you?" My answer made everyone laugh. I said: "You."

I **promise** to keep writing and speaking, if you'll keep **reading**.

Pretty well everything I do I do because of my love for you, a reader of my books or a client I have the privilege to work with. Hearing how my ideas have helped you get to personal or organizational success moves me deeply. Like the woman at a signing who shared how she read *The Monk Who Sold His Ferrari* to her husband while he succumbed to cancer on his deathbed to make him feel happier during his last moments. Or the businessman who read my *Leadership Wisdom from the Monk Who Sold His Ferrari* book and not only boosted profits but reshaped the culture so it honored human beings. Or the 18-year-old who told me that she got so inspired after reading *Who Will Cry When You Die?* that she started her own business and is now living her dreams.

I feel incredibly blessed. Why? Because I get to spend my life in service. So thank you. I'm more grateful to you than you'll ever know. I promise to keep writing and speaking, if you'll keep reading.

100

How to Live Forever

To live on in the minds and hearts of the generations who will follow you is to cheat death. To make such a difference through the way you lead and show up is to find immortality. To have a lasting impact on human lives—by being a great champion at work or a great parent at home or a great leader in your community—is to live forever.

To live on in the minds and hearts of the generations who will follow you is to cheat death.

"Impact" is one of my favorite words these days. So is "legacy." Greatness comes by beginning something that doesn't end with you. So stop worrying about death. Care more about life. What you will create today. What contribution you will make today. What person you will celebrate today. What fear you will beat today. What act of kindness you will offer today. What social ill you will remedy today. What wrong you will right today. I love these words of Archbishop Desmond Tutu: "There is no situation that is not transformable. There is no person who is hopeless. There is no set of circumstances that cannot be turned about by human beings and their natural capacity for love of the deepest sort."

To paraphrase Mel Gibson's character in *Braveheart* (one of my all-time favorite movies): "Every one of us will die. But so few of us really live." Perfect.

101

Lay Claim to Greatness

Blame or claim—that's the choice each of us has to make each day. Blame what's not working or claim the gift in the seemingly negative situation. The world needs more heroes. And heroes spend their days hunting for the best. They see the best amidst adversity. They see the best in others. They dig for the best in themselves. They claim their greatness. And in doing so, they get their best lives.

It's **never** too late to become the person you have always **dreamed** of being.

An extraordinary life is not something only available for the chosen few—people with perfect teeth and royal pedigrees. You and I are destined for greatness. We are meant to live spectacular lives. That's hardwired into our DNA. But we need to do our part to make it all happen. Choice by choice. Step by step. Small gains eventually yield giant results. Life truly does want us to win. We only need to do our part.

So lay claim to your greatness. Drive a stake into the ground to mark your place under the sun. Stop being a prisoner of your past and become the architect of your future. And remember, it's never too late to become the person you have always dreamed of being.

Resources for Personal Greatness

Sharma Leadership International offers a complete range of learning tools and coaching services to help you realize your highest potential and live an extraordinary life. Getting you to world class both in your career as well as in your personal life is our mission.

robinsharma.com
ELEVATE YOUR LIFE. TRANSFORM YOUR WORLD™

At this tremendously popular website you will find Robin's blog, free podcasts to keep you inspired and on your best game, The Robin Sharma Report (free monthly eNewsletter), daily inspirational quotes, audio learning programs available for instant download, on demand eCourses, DVDs, inspirational t-shirts as well as Robin's other books. There is also a worldwide discussion forum at **robinsharma.com** where you can exchange ideas with other people dedicated to greatness, along with a full listing of upcoming events with Robin.

TheMONTHLYCOACH®

Imagine being coached personally by Robin—every 30 days—in a cutting-edge format that keeps you on track, inspired and focused on what's most important to get to your greatest life. **The Monthly Coach®** is one of our bestselling services. Every month, you receive an idea-rich online audio presentation from Robin. You can then listen to the coaching session right on your PC or iPod—or you can burn it onto a CD and experience the learning in your car. Past sessions have included How to Craft a World-Class Life, The Energy Explosion, The Cure for Fear, The 6 Simple Steps to Work-Life Balance and Manage Your Time, Master Your Life. This is a revolutionary coaching program for only $19.95 a month. To subscribe, visit **robinsharma.com** now.

**The AWAKENING
BEST SELF WEEKEND**™

Once a year, people from all around the world attend one of the most remarkable and powerful personal development workshops they will ever attend. **The Awakening Best Self Weekend™ (ABS)** is a transformational experience that will help you triumph over your fears, reconnect with your highest potential, get clarity on what you want your life to stand for and discover a life-changing system that will help you be your very best. **ABS** works (and is also one of the most fun learning experiences you'll ever have.) For more details and to register for the next **ABS** Weekend, come and visit **robinsharma.com** today. This program offers resources for Organizational Greatness Class Leaders along with content-rich, engaging training manuals for each of your employees.

Free Audio Download for Readers of *The Greatness Guide*

Robin has a gift for you. To help you get to your greatness quickly, you can now listen to Extraordinary Leadership for free—one of Robin's most popular audio programs (retail value $24.95 USD). In this thought-provoking, potent and practical presentation, you will learn unique ideas to get you to world class, both in your career and within your life. Simply visit **robinsharma.com** and download your free copy. We only ask one thing of you: that you share this program with others so that, together, we can positively impact many lives.

Resources for Organizational Greatness

"In this time of dazzling change, global competition and tremendous uncertainty, the organizations that will lead the field will be those that grow and develop the leadership capabilities of each of their employees faster than their competition." Robin Sharma

 Grow The Leader™ is a revolutionary and strikingly powerful training program that helps employees lead without title and organizations get to world class. Many of the world's best-known companies are using Grow The Leader™ to develop leadership cultures, realize the highest performance potential of their staff, unleash innovation and create an extraordinary team that wins in their market.

Based on The 8 Best Practices of World Class Leaders, **Grow The Leader™** will help your people:
- think, feel and behave like world class leaders.
- focus their actions on activities that create spectacular results.
- show personal responsibility, renewed passion and lasting engagement.
- become superb team players that collaborate and help the organization succeed.
- seize the opportunities change presents.
- awaken natural creativity and talent for innovation to drive constant improvement.
- discover what the best performers in business do to achieve work-life balance and show personal leadership.

Essentially, **Grow The Leader™** is a train-the-trainer program. You identify people within your organization who you want trained in the process. One of our certified **GTL Master Coaches™** will then train these individuals to facilitate **Grow The Leader™** workshops at your organization. You also get

Grow The Leader™ DVDs with Robin Sharma teaching The 8 Best Practices of World-Class Leaders, along with content-rich, engaging training manuals for each of your employees.

For more information on how **Grow The Leader™** and our other resources can get your organization to world class, visit **robinsharma.com** or call us today at (905) 889-7900.

Presentations with Robin Sharma

Keynote Speeches and Leadership Workshops

Robin Sharma is one of the most in-demand speakers and workshop leaders in the world today. His leadership ideas have helped many organizations get to world class and have shown employees in over 40 countries how to lead without title and realize their best. His presentations are deeply inspiring, idea-rich and full of real-world tactics that your staff can immediately apply to get them and your organization to greatness. For more information on Robin's presentations, visit **robinsharma.com** or contact us at (905) 889-7900.

The**ELITE**PERFORMERS**SERIES** WORKSHOP™

The Elite Performers Series Workshop™ is a groundbreaking two-day leadership program designed to help your people learn the habits of leadership and discover what the best performers in business do to get their outstanding results. It is unique, highly engaging and "learning made fun." Most importantly—it works. Organizations all over the world have been transformed by **The Elite Performers Series Workshop™**. And after your team has experienced **The Elite Performers Series Workshop™**, you can enrol them in **The Elite Performers Series Advanced™**—a full year of leadership coaching with Robin Sharma or one of his **Certified Master Coaches™**. For more information, visit **robinsharma.com** or call us today at (905) 889-7900.

Give the gift of
GREATNESS